Brian's writing is always hilarious and clever (if you haven't read his first book, what the hell are you waiting for?) but in his latest memoir about writing cartoons with his dad he also captures the beauty, nuance, and complexity of the father-son relationship. Another must read!

—Stefanie Wilder-Taylor,
author of *Sippy Cups Are Not for Chardonnay*

This excellent book is about the complicated but loving relationship between a father and a son. It's about the healing power of creativity. Plus: funny cartoons! So really, there's no excuse not to buy it.

—A.J. Jacobs,
author of *Thanks A Thousand: A Gratitude Journey*

Praise for
Hyper-Chondriac

"Frazer's first book is the perfect medicine for anyone suffering from a case of treacly-memoir syndrome. Hilarious and biting, Hyper-Chondriac recounts the author's lifelong battle with various ailments and maladies, ranging from minor instances of frostbite to rage-filled meltdowns. Frazer's reflections are distinct and laugh-out-loud funny. During a teen rendezvous, Frazer contemplates how his date, suffering from scoliosis, removes her brace: "It probably had to involve her entire family, as if they were an Indy pit crew." It's that kind of spiked, wickedly funny observation that makes this sickness-filled book so easy to swallow. A-"

—Entertainment Weekly

"...caustically funny yet quietly moving..."

—USA Today

"How did Brian Frazer take his neuroses and write a hysterical book, while mine just annoy my family? Seriously, this is one funny book. Damn it."

—Ray Romano

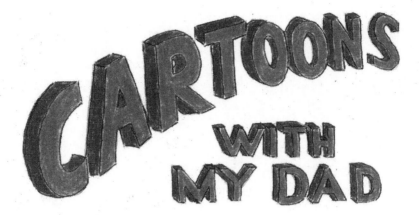

Brian Frazer

Illustrated by Sam Frazer

New Galleon

Los Angeles   California

Published by

New Galleon, an imprint of Genius Book Publishing

31858 Castaic Road, #154

Castaic, CA 91384

Library of Congress Control Number: 2019936900

ISBN: 978-1-947521-09-4

First Edition — Standard

Printed in the United States of America

Table of Contents

CHAPTER 1
SUPERHERO

Hicksville, New York
1977

Clunk. Clunk. Clunk.

The elevator was out of service, so my father dragged the dark blue hand truck up the stairs to the top of the Long Island Railroad platform.

Clunk. Clunk. Clunk.

The bouncing from each concrete step made the elastic cord securing the two tomato cartons filled with comic books look as if it would snap any second. If it didn't hold there would be Captain Marvels, Sub-Mariners, Smokey Stovers, Green Lanterns, Human Torches, Captain Americas and Pogos strewn all over the grimy station. I followed two or three steps behind him just in case it did.

Clunk. Clunk. Clunk.

"Dad, how come we never drive into the city?"

"Because this is easier," my father, Sam, insisted. He also insisted on wearing his Justice League of America jacket, a Mighty Thor baseball cap and a large silver ring with the Superman "S" on his sausage-like finger.

"How is it easier?"

"This way we don't have to look for parking in Manhattan."

"Yeah but if we drove we wouldn't have to drag the comics up all these stairs, then take a train into Penn Station, then drag all the comics up some more stairs," I said. My scrawny arms were already tired as I lugged the large canvas bag containing my father's over-sized thermos filled with black coffee, the Sunday newspaper and way too many bagels for the two of us.

"Believe me," said the sweaty forty-four-year-old with the Fred MacMurray face and Popeye forearms. "This is easier." My father had seemingly studied the issue from every angle.

Technically he was right, because navigating the thirty-two miles into New York by car would have taken us hours. My father was petrified to drive on the highway, so we would have taken side streets the entire way. And because I was thirteen, still three years away from a learner's permit, I was unqualified to drive on any surface.

Instead, we sat on the train for the forty-minute trip as my father surreptitiously sketched passengers on a pad with a charcoal pencil in between taking hits on his inhaler. Meanwhile, I leafed through the sports section while eyeballing his stash of comics like a hawk in case anyone tried any shenanigans. And, if anyone did, my father would have a damn good sketch of him[1].

Although selling comics wasn't what he did for a living—he was a first-grade teacher—my father had always wanted to be a cartoonist. Art was in his blood.

---

1   Or her. Females steal, too.

My father, age 5, looking like a very tiny JFK

His childhood friend, Chopsey[2], said the two of them were obsessed with discovering new museums throughout New York City and that my father always had a love of art. "By the time Sam was in first grade," Chopsey told me, "he had already mastered perspective. In fact, he designed an elaborate forty-panel cartoon written on a giant scroll for their classroom. Ambitious for a first grader? That's an understatement." In the late 1940s, my dad commuted from Brooklyn to the High School of Industrial Arts[3] on Manhattan's Upper East Side. After graduating from Pratt Institute with a degree in Art Education, he became an elementary school art teacher to pay the bills. In the interim, he had a modicum of artistic success. He had an exhibit of his oil paintings at Queens College

---

2   My father hadn't spoken to Chopsey since college. They hadn't had a falling out, just lost touch. I'd never met Chopsey and my father had no photos of him, so I called Chopsey. He lived in St. Louis and was a successful professor involved in engineering. I'm still kicking myself that I didn't ask him why his nickname was Chopsey. My father didn't remember.

3   I would have added the word "prestigious" but that sounds pretentious.

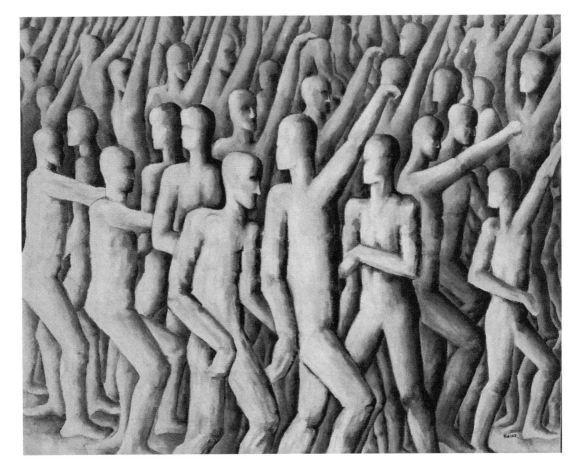

One of my father's oil paintings from the Queens College exhibit

and was often commissioned to do calligraphy and pen and ink drawings of photographs from bar mitzvahs, weddings, and family gatherings.

I wondered if art was in my blood, too. During the bicentennial—with a little guidance from my dad—I won my sixth-grade art contest. First prize was repainting my entry in the school's hallway outside the gym. The mural took me a total of sixteen after-school hours to complete.

My dad had no input on the catchy slogan

It filled me with pride that my mural would live on for years, if not decades, for future students to see. Then, two weeks later, the school year ended, and bulldozers appeared in the parking lot. That summer, the entire building was torn down—soon to be replaced by retirement homes. I felt deceived. The prize should have been a trophy or a plaque, not something that would be destroyed days after the paint had dried. In hindsight I wish I had finished second.

As our train inched towards Manhattan, I beamed as I angled my body to absorb the reflection in the window of my new pride and joy—my custom denim jacket with the album cover of Gerry Rafferty's *City to City* on the back. I had asked my father to paint it on for me in the summer in hopes it would make me popular in my first year in middle school as a seventh grader. The art was flawless. My popularity spike? Negligible at best. Bruce Hastings liked the colors, Linda Maruzzi once gave me a head nod when she sat in back of me, John Bambus thought I was even lamer now because Gerry Rafferty was no Pink Floyd.

The album cover I loved so much I had my dad paint it on my back
where I could never see it without the help of glass

Nonetheless, there was a certain smugness every time I put on that jacket. "*My father* painted this, damnit!" I'd silently say to myself as I slid each of my arms through.

When we got to our destination—the ballroom of the McAlpin Hotel—my dad exchanged greetings with the other sellers. Everyone seemed to know him. His twenty-two-page catalogue[4] was available by mail for a dollar—which with any purchase, the customer would get his dollar refunded. He had also been one of the first dealers to advertise in the back of the Overstreet Price Guide, a thick paperback that determined the value of every comic in existence.[5] It was the Kelly Blue Book for superheroes. Once Mr. Overstreet actually called our house to ask my father a question about comics, which was the equivalent of a writer getting a call from Merriam-Webster. I remember the thrill when I answered the phone, heard the caller's name, then covered the receiver with one hand and yelled for my father to pick up the phone. "It's Bob Overstreet!" My father was officially famous-adjacent.

My dad began removing the comics from the cartons, pure impulse dictating which ones were worthy of display underneath the thick sheet of plastic that would soon cover them to prevent theft. Only the lucky ones in the front row had their entire covers visible; the rest overlapped so only the top third of the book (little more than the title) was revealed.

As my father picked up each comic—each housed in a snug plastic bag with a round green sticker on it where the price was written—he studied them as if flashing back to his childhood.

"I remember when I bought this at the corner store," he said, holding Action Comics #21 aloft.

"Was that one of the ones that grandma threw out?" Actually, my grandmother, a clean freak, had thrown all of them out. She got rid of a few at a time until her only son's collection was more of a selection. And soon any trace of a comic was gone from their Brownsville, Brooklyn apartment.

---

4   He would pay me a penny for each one I collated and stapled.

5   Bob Overstreet could have bought a comic worth a dollar, then declared its value at $300,000 in his next Price Guide. It was the closest thing to printing money.

"Do you know how much all those comics would have been worth if grandma hadn't thrown them out?"

"Um… 75 cents?" I said, being a wise-ass jerk-face knucklehead.

"Tens of thousands of dollars."[6]

Part of the reason my dad started re-collecting comic books was that he thought he could recoup some of the financial carnage his mother had inflicted on him. He also wanted to rekindle his extremely happy childhood. (Well, extremely happy when his mother wasn't throwing away all his stuff behind his back.)

"Brian, watch the table. I'm going to take a look around." Yes, he just entrusted me with thousands of dollars of comics. Then again, I was his son and there weren't any cell phones back then to distract a teenager. Besides, I was the only candidate in the family up to this task. My other three siblings couldn't have cared less about comics or sacrificing half of their weekends. Mark, 20, and Debbie, 19, were in college and no longer living at home, and Stacey, 8, was more interested in dollhouses.

Oddly enough, for all the time I spent around comic books, I wasn't an avid reader of them. When I did indulge, I gravitated towards the vintage Disney titles like Mickey Mouse, Donald Duck and, later, Uncle Scrooge. Perhaps the reason I wasn't into the superhero genre was because my father insisted on dressing like one. His Justice League jacket was such a staple of his wardrobe that when he took it off it was like looking at Lincoln without his beard and top hat.

Anyway, I was used to eccentricity. I was growing up in a house where I made all my calls from inside a 1931 phone booth and watched television seated in a 1903 barber chair. We had a jukebox from 1938 that my parents played whenever they wanted to impress someone, an antique merry-go-round horse in our living room, and a second jukebox from the early '60s that I played whenever it was my turn to impress someone.

Once my dad had left his Superman ring on our bathroom sink. When I brought it to him in the kitchen, he flopped to the floor, got on his hands and

---

6   Which meant hundreds of thousands today. Or billions of dollars if you're reading this in the year 2147.

knees, and crawled towards me, saying, "So... weak ... without... ring... need... it... to... be... powerful... again...."

On the days when we'd sold a lot of comics, the train ride home felt as if we had just won the World Series. When we hadn't, my dad never sulked, never got down. There was always something positive to focus on.

"I traded business cards with that Swenson man. He lives in Queens. We might work out a big trade in the next few weeks. He's really into Pogo and Li'l Abner."

We usually didn't get home until six or seven and it was always fun to try to fool my mother with our poker faces as to how our day went.

"How'd it go?" My mother, Rhoda, an Audrey Hepburn doppelganger with high cheekbones and deep brown eyes, already had an inkling—just not a final tally. My father would sporadically march out to a pay phone in the hotel lobby—his baggy pants jingling with change—and give her updates throughout the day.

"Not so good," he would say glumly.

"Terrible," I'd add for dramatic effect.

Then we'd turn to each other and start giggling and spill the beans.

"Dad sold $800 worth of Spider-Mans to this one guy from Delaware!"

"Yep. We also exchanged cards. He might be interested in even more!"

My mother was just as excited as we were.

My father and I would make this pilgrimage into the city on a monthly basis, just the two of us. We enjoyed every second of it.

And then:

In the fall of 1977, my mom was diagnosed with multiple sclerosis. I don't remember her ever being sick before. She was healthy one day and permanently ill the next.

My father and mother met on a double blind date in 1952 in Sheepshead Bay. He was nineteen, she seventeen. They were Brooklyn Jews who loved to read, laugh, and watch old movies. My mother collected antiques—jukeboxes, pharmacy signs, movie posters, anything from the '20s, '30s and '40s—while my father was also a baseball yearbook aficionado. They worked as elementary school teachers in the same district, commuting together for twenty years. But once her health went, it seemed they had nothing in common except their address.

My mother's easygoing, nurturing attitude was devoured by the disease; her sense of humor and patience became extinct. She lost the ability to drive, walk, or put on her clothes. It must have been humiliating. Our arts and crafts projects making animals out of pom-poms, back-to-school shopping at Macy's, and regular visits to Hamburger Choo-Choo—in which a small train with plates balanced on it carried your burger around the counter and *stopped in front of your exact seat!*—were no longer enjoyable because it was only a question of how many times my mother would snap at us in frustration. In 2018, I had a double-hernia operation and the first couple of days after surgery I was in excruciating pain. I was beyond cranky and yelly and constipated and barely mobile and kind of hated everyone and everything. However, I knew that, even if I were to recover on the slow end of things, in a week or two I would feel completely better. My mother lived this daily existence of torture and heartbreak with zero chance things would ever improve forever. She lived without hope. In fact, if she were lucky her condition would just remain the same and not get worse. It was perfectly natural that 21 Adrienne Drive was transformed into a vortex of screaming and yelling and misery as my dad tried to care for his kids and disabled wife.

The odds of my father ever becoming a professional cartoonist were now a thousand Long Island Expressway exits beyond remote. Any chance of a painting career for him vanished. It was nearly impossible for him to focus on his craft. Acrylics would often dry before he returned to his easel after helping my mother get dressed or fed or use the bathroom, and navigating the complexities of oils required concentration the constant interruptions wouldn't permit. Actually, there wasn't time for anything. Even after he became an "empty nester," my father was rarely away from the house for more than a half-hour. If you tied a five-mile long rope to our house and the other end to the tailpipe of my dad's red Volkswagen Beetle there would always be slack.

He rushed through errands as if he were being timed on an obstacle course. On the rare occasion he and I went out to a restaurant we'd have such a quick meal it felt like we were training for the Nathan's hotdog eating contest.

My father was by nature chatty and gregarious with a dry sense of humor, but now spent the majority of his time as his new alter ego, Monotone Man, his deep baritone voice eking out the bare minimum of words without inflection. And, because of these new responsibilities to my mother, he no longer had time for friends. The extent of his social life became making small talk at the local post office, deli counter, and pharmacy. For my siblings and me, it got harder to connect with him; his preoccupation with my mother's health and the toll of being a constant caretaker—"full-time" didn't come close to describing his obligation to caring for my mother—made him distant and aloof. No more train trips, no more comic book shows. Our long talks turned into sound bites.

As a teenager, I would often go with him on errands—to pick up burgers, mail a comic he had just sold via his catalogue or go grocery shopping—just to steal a bonding moment or two. But, even freed from the turmoil of the house, he had become so distracted he no longer lived in the present—a habit I was soon to pick up. My father only had time to think about the immediate future—and that future was as monotonous as his voice—he had to get home as quickly as possible to attend to my mother.

I saw the wear and tear on his face and body as the love of his life was slowly hijacked by a disease neither of them could control or even understand. As her sole caretaker for decades, my father had to repeatedly transport her rapidly expanding body (courtesy of nearly a half-century of declining health and inertia) from bed to wheelchair to bathroom to wheelchair and back to bed as many as fifteen times a day. And that didn't take into account the numerous doctor appointments in which squeezing her into a car became exceedingly difficult for his geriatric body. In fact, their weights seemed to be ballooning proportionately, either out of deference to one another or a convergence of depression. My father would routinely sit in front of the television and eat an entire half-gallon of Breyers ice cream straight out of the container as he waited patiently to know not *if* my mother would summon him for assistance, but when.

CHAPTER 2
DRAWN TOGETHER

Ft. Myers, Florida
April 2012

An ambulance arrived. An ambulance was always arriving. This time, however, it wouldn't be going to a hospital. This time it would take my mother to a nursing home. She had been ill and disabled for half of her seventy-seven years.

In 2002, out of necessity, my parents moved to the Sunshine State. Their house on Long Island—the only address I ever had before going to college—had too many stairs, not to mention that icy winters and old people don't mix. Most importantly, my older sister, Debbie, a tough bleached-blonde dynamo, was a hospice nurse in Ft. Myers. My father was reluctant to move but realized that, with no support system within a five-hour drive or more, he had little choice. Elderly couples leaving Long Island for the sun and low taxes of Florida is nothing new, but most do it voluntarily.

Once in Florida—where every house seemed (by Northeast standards) about 30% too large—a button was installed at the side of my mother's bed; otherwise her pleas for help would be inaudible through the maze of hallways and excess space. The bell delivered eight or nine notes per push and was so loud it was guaranteed to wake up even the deepest of sleepers. I could hear it while mowing the lawn. Sometimes it would ring twenty or thirty cycles a day; each time my father would race into her bedroom like a firefighter, usually completely out of breath.

"W-w-w-w-what do you need, Ro?" My father slept in a small room on the other side of the house because the master bedroom was the only one large enough to accommodate a wheelchair. It had been years since my parents had shared a bed due to my mother's frail condition.

"I need a glass of water!"

"You have a glass of water right here, Rhoda."

"I want a new glass with new water!"

And off he went to get her a different glass with different water.

My mother was demanding and beyond harsh with him. Had he been an Uber driver she would have never given him more than one star. No matter what he did, it was never exactly what she wanted or when or where she wanted it. Understandably the torrents of pain drowned out any semblance of her old self and brought out the worst in her. Taking care of my mother was a thankless task.

When I'd ask him how he was able to deal with my mother's constant demands, he'd answer, "It is the right thing to do. The status quo, as horrible as it is, is the lesser of all evils. Any other options are far more complicated and negative."

"Did mom always have a dark side before she got sick?"

"Not at all. She was sweet."

"Then how did she get so mean? Was it just because of her illness?"

"She had a rough childhood. Her parents discriminated against her. She was like Cinderella. Her brothers were all treated royally, and she had to take care of them and practically be a second mother to them."

When my mother went into the nursing home, my father's caregiving schedule remained intense. His seventy-nine-year-old back got a breather, but his dedication to her never faltered. "'Til death do us part" was his mantra.

He showed up when visiting hours started at 8 AM and stayed until he was kicked out twelve or thirteen hours later. Occasionally he'd do two shifts, driving the thirty-five minutes back home for a nap to help break up the day. My father befriended the entire staff, a bevy of robust middle-aged Jamaican women, to remind them of my mother's dietary quirks, pill schedule, and bathroom prep. Whenever he picked up a shake for her at Wendy's he'd be sure to get one for whichever nurse was on duty, too. As cantankerous as my mother was to the help, my father's excessive kindness helped my parents average out to one normal person.

A month after my mother's relocation, I flew in from Los Angeles to visit. The good news was that the nursing home staff had taken most of the actual heavy lifting off my father's plate. The bad news was that when my mother was sleeping—unlike being at home where my dad had all his accoutrements—there was nothing for him to do. I saw the sea of empty time he faced, especially with her erratic sleep schedule. Inside the stark room, seconds felt like minutes and minutes like hours.

While my father's days were beyond predictable, mine were anything but that. At forty-eight, I lived with the uncertainty of where I would get my next job. For the prior three decades, I had made my money doing stand-up and then writing for television and magazines. However, the magazine industry was dying, internet writing paid a fraction of what magazines did, television work was erratic, and—unless you spent half your time on the road—stand-up would barely pay a gas bill, let alone a mortgage. I was desperately trying to figure out how to make ends meet in the second half of my life. I considered applying to Starbucks except a) at my age with no coffee-making experience I probably wouldn't get hired; and b) I feared seeing people on the other side of the partition who knew me. My self-esteem was already in a precarious position to begin with.

I was hoping to be a late-bloomer but then I remembered that I had already bloomed. I won the Boston Comedy Riot at twenty-two, made my first national television appearance at twenty-three on MTV (I went on in between a couple of fellas named Adam Sandler and David Spade), earned a master's degree in business communications at twenty-four and landed a semi-lucrative Hollywood writing job on MAD TV at thirty-one. I'd also written eleven songs and then flown to England—without knowing a single musician or producer—and recorded a punk album with a band at thirty-two.[7] However, it had been years since anything notable had happened to me. My memoir *Hyper-Chondriac: One Man's Quest to Hurry Up and Calm Down* had been published by Simon and Schuster back in 2007. My father knew of my struggles to have a purpose over the past decade, but it was never something we spoke about. He was aware that I had chosen a tough field in which to make a living.

My wife, Nancy, was also aware. We had met writing thought-bubbles on the television show *Blind Date* in 2000 and I knew ten minutes into our first drink that we would marry—which we did about a year and a half later. She was (and still is) a petite brunette from the East Coast with a biting sense of humor and there has never been a second when I wasn't convinced she was my soul mate. My temperamental opposite, she also experienced the ebbs and flows of work in the business so she knew we weren't in an industry that provided much stability. Rarely was one guaranteed more than thirteen weeks of work before a contract was up or the show one was working on would be cancelled.

I always carried around a small notebook in which I jotted down ideas and then assigned a medium for each. For instance, "magazine article," "stand-up," "movie treatment," etc. As I sat at my mother's bedside, I heard a patient yell at a relative of theirs that they were "being micro-managed." I said to myself, "I wonder if one-celled organisms under a microscope complained about being 'micro micro-managed'?" I scribbled it down in my book, thinking I might find a way to use it later.

My father came in with my mother's shake from Wendy's and, sensing she was particularly tense, went to his default strategy of trying to make her laugh. Which, regardless of the quality of the joke, was no easy task. He often resorted to physical comedy.

"Look, I'm a walrus!" My dad had stuck a pair of French fries between his upper lip and gums.

---

7   The name of the band was "Invasion of Privacy" and last month I received another $2.34 from Spotify streams.

"Sam, I'm not in the mood!"

My father wasn't about to give up.

"Arf arf arf!" He bleated as he clapped.

"Sam, that is not funny." A wry smile began to creep out from the corners of her mouth.

"Arf arf arf!" He repeated even louder this time.

"Sam, you're an idiot!" A normal-sized smile emerged on my mother's face as my father began to laugh at his own joke, which made me laugh too. Oh, and incidentally, being called an idiot by my mother wasn't an insult, but rather the highest praise. It was the equivalent of a comic getting a standing ovation.

A few minutes later, the flash of levity was gone; the searing pain was back and my mother was again looking for someone to blame. The nursing home staff was the logical choice.

"This place is horrible! Where is the help?!" she was on the rampage. "I rang the buzzer a long time ago!"

"Ma, you just rang it three seconds ago."

A sturdy forty-something nurse, Ranisha, entered radiating cheerful, positive energy.

"Hi, Sam. How is Rhoda doing?"

"I need something to take my pills!"

"Ro, I just brought you a shake."

"I don't want to take my pills with a shake!"

"Would you like an apple juice, Mrs. Frazer?"

"Fine," she grumbled unappreciatively.

Ranisha ducked out and my father tried to prevent the one-way confrontation from escalating.

"Rhoda, Ranisha is doing the best she can. Before you hit the buzzer, tell me what you need."

Since I was there this was allegedly my mother on her best behavior. I could only imagine how tough she was when it was just my dad and the staff.

On the plane back to California a thought struck me. I sent my father an email with a few terse sentences describing "MICRO MICRO-MANAGING" with one of the organisms saying to the other, "Move your cell membrane to the other end of the slide, please!" and asked if he'd be interested in drawing it. In his new life as a nursing home regular, he fluctuated between being completely overwhelmed and severely underwhelmed. I thought collaborating on cartoons might provide him a welcome diversion, a way to bridge that gap.

When I landed, there was still no response. Over the previous thirty years, the average length of a telephone call with my dad topped out at about forty seconds. He wasn't much of a phone guy and his time was so limited it seemed like the first item on his to-do list was *hang up as soon as possible*.

I called to tell him I had arrived safely on the West Coast and we had our typical truncated cookie-cutter conversation. I asked if he got my email and he acknowledged that he had. Then he added that he'd "think about it" before abruptly getting off the phone. After not hearing from him for a day or two I assumed he wasn't interested, that he was exhausted just dealing with my mother.

Two days later, I had my answer. That morning, during one of my mother's many naps, my father flipped over her plastic cafeteria-esque food tray—to convert it into a desk—and, with a standard #2 pencil cradled in his left hand, sketched an amoeba yelling at another amoeba under a microscope with the dialogue I'd provided.

He scanned and emailed it to me to see if it was what I had envisioned, and, if it were, he'd erase all the pencil lines and ink it in. I got so wound up that my hands trembled as I typed back my glowing approval.

Several hours later, my computer pinged. It was the inked-in cartoon.

MICRO MICROMANAGING

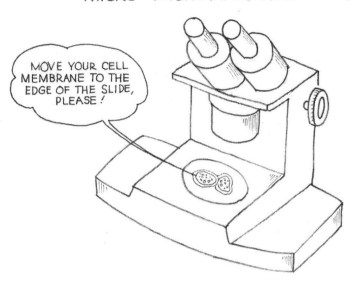

Sure, it's not the funniest cartoon ever, but I like to think of it as our Wright Brothers' Kitty Hawk. You wouldn't get in that 1903 "Flyer" now, but it was a good starting point.

I put it up on Facebook to test the waters and got eight "likes"—which felt like eight thousand. I opened up a Facebook account for my father so he could enjoy the positive feedback as well. Over speakerphone, I walked him through how to login and where to type in his password, but he didn't seem to care. I felt him disconnecting from me, as was often the case. I figured that was it. He was done. Our collaboration would be limited to a single single-panel cartoon of some single-celled organisms. That would have been a shame because our inaugural cartoon seemed to please my mother, too.

"Wanna do another one?" I figured I at least had to ask.

"I guess." Not the rousing enthusiasm I was looking for, but it was better than "no."

The following day, inspired by my mother and tapping into my father's love of superheroes, I had another idea. I called my dad, who stepped out into the hallway of the nursing home, so as not to disturb my mother's nap.

"What if we had a caption on the bottom that read, 'SUPERHEROES WHEN THEIR MOTHERS ARE AROUND'? Then we have a split screen with Batman on one side and his mother on the other side. They each have phones—not cell phones, phones with cords—in their hands and Batman is saying, 'Maaaaaa! Hang up! I'm on the Bat Phone!' and his mother quickly drops the phone back onto the receiver."

"I like that idea, but Batman was an orphan so he really didn't have a mother around." If I hadn't spent my adolescent years reading Uncle Scrooge I would've known that.

"Good point. Okay... then... what if it was Aquaman instead?" An ironic choice since neither my father nor I could swim. "And there was someone off in the distance drowning, yelling, 'Help me, Aquaman!'" I scribbled as I spoke in case anything I said was worthwhile. "Then we see Aquaman at the edge of the water, both feet still in the sand of the beach, his mother by his side. Aquaman is yelling out to the hapless drowner off in the distance, 'Sorry. Just ate. Can't go in the water for another half-hour.'"

"Can you send me an image of Aquaman when you have a chance?"

"Sure. But don't you have a lot of Aquaman comics somewhere?"

"Yes. But I prefer to work off of something on my computer screen."

"You know, it's really easy to Google Image stuff."

"It's better if you send it."

"I don't see why you can't just use your Google." Most people would have just sent it. But, unfortunately, I'm not most people. I always took the fork in the road that led to conflict and grudges, never the path of least resistance. The stubborn streak I'd inherited from my mother was hard to shed.

"You know how to use your Google," I insisted.

"You should just send it."

Seriously. Why couldn't he just use Google?!?

"Okay." I finally folded. "Speak to you tomorrow. Oh, and obviously I'll type up what we just discussed in a paragraph so you have the precise dialogue and composition."

A few days went by and no drawing arrived in my inbox. Had I offended my father with all my Google aggression? Or was he just procrastinating, as was his nature? The only other possible explanation: he forgot. He had a terrible memory. Not only would he forget birthdays, but he would always be off by a few years when asked our ages.

"Dad, did you get the paragraph and the link to Aquaman I sent?" He hadn't acknowledged my email.

"Yes."

"So how's it going?"

"It's going."

When I was a teenager my father would come to my basketball games and sit in the top row of the bleachers and sketch all the action. Drawing things that weren't in motion—like a cartoon—seemed a lot easier.

He said he couldn't show me anything yet.

"Why not, Dad?"

"I just can't."

He did offer to take a picture of the garbage can in my mother's room filled with crumpled up Aquaman drafts he'd thrown out. He didn't like the shape of Aquaman's mother's body or her nose or Aquaman's posture or the proportion of his upper body to his lower body or the shape of the thought bubbles that contained the words or the spacing between the letters in the caption on the bottom. His artistic muscles had lain dormant for decades and it was taking a while to reacquaint himself with perspective, hand-brain coordination, and the self-kindness artists require to not destroy themselves with their own sense of inadequacy.

I learned something that really shocked me: my father was a perfectionist. The only other indication of this was when he hung the antique signs that covered the walls of my childhood home. Each one was always diligently measured and re-measured so they'd be straight. If they weren't, my mother (who was also a perfectionist) would have criticized him for it. Besides, hanging a sign is basically pass/fail. It's either straight or it isn't. There's little room for interpretation or nuance. Art is nothing if not nuance.

My computer pinged, and I rushed over to see if it was from my father. Nope. More spam. Those Goldstar people are relentless! One Arctic Monkeys concert at the Hollywood Bowl doesn't mean I want to see Live Magic at Black Rabbit Rose. An hour later, I received another ping. This time, his email arrived, with an attachment. I couldn't wait to see it.

I would have to wait to see it. It was just a blank white rectangle. My father had put the cartoon face-up instead of facedown on the scanner. But when I called to let him know he was already in the car on the way to the nursing home. He wouldn't be able to re-scan until the end of the day after visiting hours ended.

It was worth the wait.

SUPER HEROES WHEN THEIR MOTHERS ARE AROUND

I was amped up but, unfortunately, my Facebook friends barely seemed to notice. Just six "likes" even though in my opinion this cartoon, both in concept and execution, was far superior to our microscope.

But the number of likes didn't matter. I was hooked. I walked my dog trying to come up with cartoons. I went to the gym thinking of cartoons. I became a more attentive listener in hopes that a friend or stranger would say a word that would trigger a thought. (Incidentally, I take zero responsibility for any good idea that enters my head. It has nothing to do with me; I'm just an antenna. I do, however, take full responsibility for any bad ideas that leave my mouth or fingers.)

The following evening, I emailed my father a list of three more.

1. We see a pair of Eskimo men shivering. One says to the other, "What do you want to do today?" The other responds, "We have 260 words for snow. Let's come up with ten more!"

2. The caption on the bottom reads, "CORN BRAVERY". Then we see a piece of corn on the cob on a plate. There are a few scattered pieces of corn remaining on the cob and some random pieces on the perimeter of the plate. One tiny piece of corn on the perimeter of the plate exclaims, "I'm going back for Martha!"

3. We see Rudolph the Red-Nosed Reindeer in a hardware store. The store employee approaches him and hands him a blue bulb for his burnt-out nose as he says, "Sorry, no more red in stock. Won't get another shipment until February."

In my stand-up career I tended to not go for the obvious joke. I thought there wasn't any challenge in getting a bull's-eye from two feet away. But my counter-tactic was hitting a target that was so far away, even if I did connect, would anyone even see it? For instance, I would ask the audience if they were ready to play a game. After they applauded that they were, I'd enthusiastically announce, "Okay, try to guess which is my favorite spoon!" I'd then pull a pair of standard metal spoons from my pockets and hold each of them up individually. "How many people here think that *this* is my favorite spoon? Okay, now how many people here think that *this* is my favorite spoon?" After the clapping died down I'd calmly place both spoons back in my pockets and incredulously yell, "Are you guys NUTS!?!? You'd think I'd bring my favorite spoon to a place like this?!?!" That would usually elicit loud laughs from between three and five audience members and confused silence from everyone else. Yet I continued to do that joke night in and night out. Which is reason number 1,857,574 why you've never heard of me until twenty-two pages ago.

"Which cartoon should I do next?" my dad asked.

We strategized as if drawing up a play on the sidelines of a basketball court.[8]

"Maybe try the Rudolph first since he's a recognizable character. And people like animals."

"Okay."

"Do you need me to send you an image of a reindeer?"

"Yes."

"I wish you would just learn how to use Google. I mean all you have to do is type the word 'Google' and then once the page comes up just type whatever it is you're looking for."

"It's better if you do it."

"Why is it better if I do it?"

"It just is."

"Fine." I folded again.

By the time I woke up, this was in my inbox.

---

8   Incidentally, my father is a die-hard Knicks fan. I had no choice but to be a Nets fan because the Nassau Coliseum was accessible without taking a highway.

I was sorry I woke up.

I didn't know where to begin with my father. a) Rudolph looked like a Muppet, not a reindeer; b) Rudolph *already* had a red nose, which made a second red nose pointless; c) The dialogue should have read, "No more *red* in stock." Not "Out of stock."; and d) Whatever the clerk was holding in his hand looked like a white egg, not a blue bulb.

I hadn't yet confirmed that I received his cartoon so my father called.
"Did you get Rudolph?"
"Yeah. Kind of."
I dreaded giving him criticism. I knew he was thick-skinned and could probably take it. After all, he was criticized day-in and day-out by my mother. The issue wasn't him. I had inherited something else from my mother: a lack of bedside manner. I was unnecessarily blunt. Honest, sure. But there are ways to be honest without hurting someone's feelings. Like when Nancy says I should "take it down a notch" when she just as easily could say I'm being an ass. I took a deep breath and gently went over each of the mishaps as my father silently jotted them down one by one. He then slowly repeated everything we'd just gone over to make sure we were on the same page. The second we hung up I worried that I hadn't been gentle enough. The last thing he needed was more tension in his life. After not hearing from him for hours, I assumed that my abrasiveness had repelled him.

When my computer pinged that evening, it was an attachment from my father that, I figured would just be the scribbled words "I'M DONE WITH YOUR NONSENSE!" Fortunately, my paranoia was off. The attachment was perfect.

I continued to email him ideas and dialogue daily, he'd pencil it in, scan it back to me, and then we'd discuss any changes before he did the final inking and, when appropriate, added color. Sometimes we'd speak two or three times a day until we were both happy with the cartoon.

At forty-eight and seventy-nine, my dad and I were sketching out a new life together.

CHAPTER 3
ALONE

CORN BRAVERY

The nursing home could no longer accommodate my mother's rapidly declining condition so she was transferred to hospice care. We didn't expect her to be there longer than six months. Later that day, Debbie called and said my mother had the death rattle, so I jumped on a plane to see her for the last time. I was changing planes in Dallas at 6:10 am when I got the voice mail. She had spent all of eight hours in hospice care before her body quit. For the past four decades she'd been talking about how she wanted to die because of all the pain and frustration and loss of independence and helplessness and humiliation and now, at 77, she had gotten her wish.

It was tough to remember the last time I'd seen her genuinely cheerful. It was probably in 1986 at my college graduation weekend when she and my dad came up to Boston to see me perform at a comedy club. The ordeal just for her to get down the stairs of the basement venue—left arm locked with my dad's, right arm clutching the handrail, legs inoperable—must have felt like tightrope walking between two skyscrapers. I was touched by her efforts. Coincidentally, it's also the last time I can remember my mother having alcohol—a lone Bailey's and Kahlua. I had a good set that night and my mother couldn't have looked prouder. Although, had I bombed I'm sure she would have been just as proud and blamed a poor response on the audience. After the show I watched—even more proudly than she had watched me—as she hobbled back up the steps, 300% happier than when she had descended them. I wish there were more of these memories.

Her death was still more abrupt than I had imagined. Part of me was relieved she wouldn't suffer another minute but part of me wanted to say goodbye in person. However, my sister said that it was better the way it happened—from a distance. In her last days, my mother was even more irritable and demanding than usual.

Listening to the message for a second time felt even more surreal than the first. My body felt hollow, my head empty, I could almost feel each of the beats of my heart as if it were trying to remind me that I was still alive.

My thoughts quickly shifted to my father. For years we had been planning on him dying first, due to all the rigors of my mother's illness. My father had dated "a handful of women" but none since 1952. He'd never shared a bed with anyone other than my mother. He'd never been alone. And now, at eighty, he was stuck in Florida living in perpetual air conditioning to combat the oppressive humidity, 1,300 miles from Long Island where at least he was comfortable in the neighborhood and knew some of the people.

My dad picked me up at the Ft. Myers airport. Even though her death was just three and a half hours ago, he looked exhausted, like he hadn't slept in weeks. He was disheveled, even more overweight and appeared as if he had just emerged from a long battle, technically victorious but in reality just slightly less of a loser than the loser. On the fifteen-minute ride from the airport to the house, my father went from a man of few words to a man of none.

I thought back to all the hours of awkward silences we'd had in cars over the years; driving from Long Island to Brooklyn to see his parents, often without a sound except for horrible Muzak on the AM car radio or the constant loop of WINS news repeating the same stories every fifteen minutes. When he was teaching me how to drive I remember nervously asking him, "Dad, which is more important? The cars in the rearview mirror or the cars in front of me?" "Both," he replied. And that was the end of that conversation. But this silence was worse because I had no idea if it would end after we parked.

When we arrived back at his house, it looked as if a bomb had gone off inside. Even under the most optimal of conditions, my father and cleanliness had an adversarial relationship. In fact, the reason the house even looked this good was because Debbie—who *is* a neat freak—would come by and clean it every few days.

"Dad, do you need me to do anything?" I meant besides battle this cauldron of filth—which was a given.

"No."

"What do you mean, no? There are a lot of things that have to be done."

"I have to call the cemetery and make arrangements."

"Let me help."

"Once I have a precise time you can make the airline reservations."

My mother was being buried on Long Island where my parents had pre-paid for a plot years ago. I have no idea where I'll be buried or if I'll be buried. As far as I'm concerned whatever someone wants to do with my body when I'm gone is fine.

"Will you be okay with flying?" I worried he would be too nervous to even get on a plane. My dad had a staggering number of unusual neuroses. In addition to being afraid to drive on highways, he was also terrified to drive over any bridge and would pull over and make someone else in the car switch seats, drive over it for him, then switch back and resume his steering duties on the other side. When it was time for me to go to college, instead of driving me and my things up to Boston he hired a stranger with a van out of the local PennySaver to do it. That's right. A stranger. With a van. From the precursor to Craig's List. Who brought with him his chain-smoking girlfriend who took the only other bolted down seat up front. This relegated me to sit in a folding chair in the back of the van with my stuff as I slid around like an air hockey puck for six hours. My dad didn't even bother to vet the man's packing abilities as he placed my stereo at the top of a large stack of towels. Seriously, who lets a stranger drive their kid 220 miles? And without a seatbelt? Apparently my father's fear of highways dwarfed his fear of having his son kidnapped.

"If you're more comfortable I can rent a car and drive you there, Dad."

"That won't be necessary. I can fly." He had been on exactly one plane in the past twenty-five years—the one that brought him to Florida.

"Okay. I'll book the tickets. And I'll take care of the hotel arrangements." Despite being the king of the procrastinators, my father wanted this funeral done as soon as possible—and not just because of the Jewish tradition. But first we had to arrange for my mother's body to be transported.

His house was eerily quiet, but since my mother had moved into the nursing home, my father was now used to coming back to an empty place. It was odd for me not hearing my mother's buzzer go off every half-hour or so. I wondered if my father would ever adjust to the blaring silence.

"Are you planning to look for a new house, Dad?" Maybe the question was a little premature but I had to ask.

"Why would I need a new house?"

"Because this one is pretty big for one person. Plus, y'know... the memories... you might want a fresh start."

"I'm not interested in moving."

It was 500 square feet larger than the house that six of us and a series of large Old English Sheepdogs had occupied on Long Island.

"Are you thinking about getting a dog?"

"I would love to but I don't want to have to take care of anything else right now."

He then defrosted a bagel in the microwave and sat and ate while reading the newspaper, his left elbow perched on the kitchen table; his left hand pressed against his jaw line—exactly how I look when I eat and read at my kitchen table. Boy, do I hate when Nancy points out that I eat like that. Which is pretty much all the time. He and I also each clear our throats with the same regularity and cadence; the only difference being it drives me crazy when he does it and my father tolerates the noise when it's me.

I tried to initiate a dialogue and repeatedly got back nothing. I was wondering if he was keeping his feelings bottled up or, conversely, if his absence of feelings *were* his feelings. Was there just a bunch of white noise filling up his skull? Or were there such a flurry of thoughts and ideas that it was impossible to collect and relay them to anyone? Then I decided to cut him some slack and hoped his need to regroup like this was just halftime of a game. Except it was way later in the game. More like a minute or two left in the fourth quarter.

Debbie came over and seemed more concerned about the level of cleanliness than my father's mental state.

"You can't eat like that!" she said in her thick Long Island accent that seemed more nasally than usual. "You gotta clean that kitchen table! That's disgusting! There's newsprint all over it!"

"This way when he recycles the paper he can read anything he missed on the table," I replied for him.

Debbie ignored me. "When is Mark coming in?"

"Who knows?" my dad answered. Mark was always running late, an odd quality for a morning DJ where every minute is mapped out to the second. It wouldn't have shocked any of us if he had missed his flight from Pittsburgh. It also made no sense to fly down to Florida and then back up to Long Island but who was I to manage my 57-year-old brother's itinerary?

Stacey, a special needs educator, was driving to Long Island from Vermont. Which wasn't surprising because she was terrified to fly and would always take the train with her two young kids from Burlington to Florida—24 hours on Amtrak vs. 2 ½ hours on Delta.[9]

Debbie sniffed, blew her nose, then sniffed again. As a nurse, she was always around germs.

"Deb are you sick?"

"I have a sinus thing. I'm not sure if I'm allowed to fly."

"Then don't."

"I have to. I'll feel terrible if I miss it."

"Are you kidding me? You've taken care of mom and dad down here for ten years. There's nothing to feel terrible about." I had no idea how anyone could do what a nurse did. On my morning hikes I often saw this elderly man with his dog—we had never exchanged more than a wave or the word "hello." Anyway, the man had suffered a stroke and fallen down the side of a mountain. He wound up in a nursing home/rehabilitation center. Because he had no family, I felt that the least I could do was show up and keep him company a few times. One day he asked me to put his socks on for him. I did, but it was probably one

9   Yes, Stacey packs a lot of fear into her 4'10" frame.

of the three toughest things[10] I'd ever done in my life. Even if nurses got paid what NBA stars were, I still couldn't be one.

I walked into my father's office and saw the stack of emails I'd sent, each one a description of a new cartoon printed out on a separate sheet of paper patiently waiting to be brought to life. Next to these was his comic book collection, which he had been downsizing—in part to help pay for my mother's exorbitant medical costs. I hoped that one day our stack of cartoons would exceed his stacks of comics.

The phone rang. It was my brother, Mark, who needed to be buzzed through the security gate. A security gate that should have had air quotes around the security part because if you were determined to penetrate the premises you could merely get out of your car then walk around the wooden barrier that barely covered the width of a Fiat.

Mark was exhausted. He was always exhausted, despite the perpetual funneling of Mountain Dew, Pepsi and Coke down his esophagus. With his brown eyes and dark hair he looked quite a bit like my mother. The rest of us had blond hair and blue/green eyes and resembled my father. Mark also brought enough luggage to go to Europe for a month.

"Hey, gang." Mark went over to hug my father. He was the lone hugger in our family and, for some reason, exulted in chest-to-chest contact. "How ya feeling, Dad?"

"As expected. You can go and rest in the guest room, Mark," my father offered. The only other option was to use my mother's narrow, twin-sized hospital bed in her bedroom—which would have been a little creepy, like one step up from napping in a coffin.

We decided that we would all meet for dinner at the local tavern, imaginatively named *The Tavern*, where the salads are iceberg, the dressings creamy and everyone is forced to shout over the way-louder-than-it-needs-to-be classic rock.

"C'mon, we have to go!" my father urged Mark and me.

---

10   The other two being passing 10th grade Geometry and not strangling the chain-smoking woman in the front seat of the van that drove me up to college.

"Seriously, what's the rush?"

"Because we told Debbie and Jon five o'clock." Jon, Debbie's husband of thirty-plus years, was a former nuclear pharmacist who had to retire in his early fifties after he went blind. Yes, my sister's life was a hoot.

"Well, let's call them up and tell them six."

"No. Let's go." My father was determined to get there at five sharp.

He insisted on driving the mile there. My father was somehow a better driver at eighty than he was at forty. Now he drove at exactly the speed limit and didn't worry about evaluating the other drivers. When I was growing up he would honk at any car that didn't signal. And not just a little honk, either. A long drawn out honk held down for what seemed five times longer than the final piano chord in *A Day in the Life*. I was embarrassed 100% of the time and urged my father to stop. He wouldn't. "You know it's illegal to make a turn without signaling," he would remind me incessantly. "Even if it's just pulling into your driveway." Honk! Hooooooonk!!!!! I still struggle with this horrible habit he programmed into my malleable teenboy skull. I find it next-to-impossible not to use my horn for even the smallest of things. Nancy is scared that one day I'm going to get shot for it. And I don't disagree. It's become so reflexive that I think the only way to break the habit is to glue barbed wire onto the center of my steering wheel so any horn usage will result in a penalty of blood and a tetanus shot.

Unfortunately, in order to get inside *The Tavern*, customers have to walk through a patio where it's evidently mandatory that everyone smokes and is required to blow the smoke into each new customer's face as one walks past. Wow, do I hate Florida. My poor father.

After we crossed through cancer gulch, the place was empty inside. Of course it was empty. It was five o'clock on a Monday!

"Phew, glad we beat the 5:02 rush, Dad."

From the moment we sat down on the wooden benches in the booth everything seemed to speed up, as if the manager was holding down the fast forward button because we were time-sharing the table with a family who would arrive at 5:30. The energy coming out of my father's silent, motionless body indicated he wanted to eat as quickly as possible then get in the car and break the sound barrier driving home.

"This feels so surreal," said my brother.

My mother's death was the toughest on Mark. Probably because, being the oldest child, he was already out of the house and in college when she got sick so he had the least jarring childhood with the peak number of "normal" years. He had the happiest memories of my mom and was in denial about her erratic behavior. Debbie, Stacey and I knew the extent of the verbal and physical abuse. My father often had to wear long-sleeved shirts in the summer because she scratched his arms up so much. Mark was insistent that things were never "that bad."

"I wish I would have gotten down here in time to say goodbye," Mark said.

"You wouldn't have wanted to, believe me," Debbie replied.

"I'm just glad she didn't suffer too much. I mean, obviously she suffered for years but... I mean... you know what I mean," I stammered.

"It is what it is," Debbie proclaimed. It was her favorite slogan, neck and neck with "Don't sweat the small stuff and it's all small stuff."

My father sat on the end of the bench, his left arm dangling off the end of the table, as he stared silently off into the distance, waiting for his food to appear.

"I remember when your sister told your mother that she was going to the Bahamas with her friend Lisa—" Jon would tell this same story whenever my mother's name came up.

"—And then your mother eventually found out that Debbie actually went there with me. She was pretty pissed off." We'd all heard this ad nauseum but at least he was trying.

My father had made the ultimate sacrifice for my mother's health. It seemed like his entire life was comprised of sacrifice. Sacrificed his art career, sacrificed his health, sacrificed his back, even sacrificed his teaching career since he had to retire early to take care of her. For a moment, out of my peripheral vision it appeared as if my dad had just slashed his wrist. I whirled my head around and was relieved that it was just a sloppily dunked French fry that had dripped ketchup onto his arm.

"We'll take the check, please," my father told the waitress. None of us had yet taken a second bite of our food. It was like hailing another cab the moment you had stepped out of a cab. No wonder I was so hyper. We were all shackled to time.

"Have you looked over the will?" Mark asked.

"Of course." Debbie was in charge of it. The big question I had: Did my mother leave him in debt? And not just from her medical bills and nursing home expenses. Because my mother was handicapped she couldn't really go out to malls so she became a mail-order addict. Back on Long Island she bought so many antiques signs and vintage movie posters from catalogues that you couldn't even tell what color our walls were. Her obsession with buying knickknacks and clothes— the latter invariably the wrong size, shape or color—meant my father, in his limited time, had to pack it up and go to UPS or the post office almost daily. For the icing on the spending cake, my mom was a magnanimous gift giver. And everybody got a gift. The UPS man, the mailman, the plumber, her doctors, the other teachers she taught with. Her generosity was unsurpassed. She had happily re-mortgaged the house several times to help pay for our college tuitions.

The waitress tossed the check on our table. You're supposed to get a bereavement rate on a flight if you can produce a person's death certificate and prove they just died. They should have the same policy for meals. Especially this one.

I slid my Mastercard onto the table.

"Brian, you sure you got it?" Mark asked.

"Yeah. I'm working now."

"On what?"

"A weekly column for a fantasy baseball site."

I thought my father would have a follow-up question since he was a big baseball fan but I got nothing.

I paid the check and we got the hell out of there. It was 5:33.

My dad, Mark and I had a somber ride to the airport on our way to Long Island. And then... the minute we entered the terminal, a miracle occurred. My father came to life. It was as if someone ejected his old SIM card and replaced it with a stranger's.

SCENES FROM THE TRIAL OF ICARUS

Now, for whatever reason, all of my father's fears seemed to be forgotten. He embraced the new things that were happening. He was jovial. He had some pep in his step. He was chatty. Words were flowing out of his mouth, each one filled with emotion. Maybe he was overcompensating for his struggles but I didn't care what the reason was. While I was stressed about making our connecting flight in Baltimore my dad got a kick out of walking through the airport security X-ray machine, asking the TSA agent if it showed if he still had his appendix since he couldn't remember. He was blown away by all the different kinds of pretzel dipping sauces at Wetzel's and how anyone could possibly decide which one was the best with which pretzel. He started speaking with the adjacent strangers at the gate, as pleased to have a conversation as I'd ever seen him.

As he boarded the plane he marveled at the giant seats in first class, the medium seats in business and the tiny seats in coach and wondered if there should be a fourth designation where very flexible people get in the fetal position and are stacked on top of one another. Then I calmed down and tried to soak everything in, too. I felt as if I was seeing the world through the eyes of someone who had been locked in a closet since the 1980s. My dad had been in such a stifling routine for so long that he instantly found anything outside of that fascinating, as far from mundane as the average traveler would.

As he leaned back in his aisle seat, he marveled at the tiny personal television screen at his disposal inches away. He found the width and heft of the armrest mesmerizing. He thought the flight crew was charming. He grabbed his newspaper and pulled out his eyeglass case that—thanks to print on-demand—had a cartoon of ours stamped on it.

"I'm still surprised how many people don't get this cartoon," he said.

"Me too. Pretty straightforward concept."

FOR SOME REASON NO ONE IN TOWN NEEDED GLASSES

He was shocked at all the people he showed it to in Florida—at the nursing home, the bagel shop, convenience store—who had no idea what the joke was. *[Spoiler alert: all the letters in the eye chart are in alphabetical order.]* He told me he thought it was a great litmus test for judging whether or not someone was "sharp."[11] I was elated to see that every time my dad took off his glasses, or put them back on, if there were witnesses the eyeglass case provided him some momentary entertainment.

It was amazing how composed he was. The man who couldn't drive over an eight-foot high bridge without a panic attack was a picture of calm at 35,000 feet. He vacillated between reading in-flight magazines and watching *King of Queens* reruns.

Since my dad seemed occupied, I pulled out my laptop to work. Like I told Mark, I had accepted a weekly gig writing a short humor column for a fantasy baseball site—even though the money was slightly more than zero. I'd just handed in my first column the previous day and part of the job entailed responding to the comments.

11　　Neither stewardess "got it" either.

THE WORLD'S WORST SCALPER

Here's something to keep in mind. People on fantasy sports sites are only interested in one thing—advice on which players to pick up for their imaginary teams so they can win real money. Any words that don't accomplish that are just getting in their way. In any case, this was the site's first humorous non-advice column. I paid $9.99 on Gogo for an internet connection in the sky and scrolled through the comments. There appeared to be a common theme: people wanted me dead. That's right. I received numerous death threats—for a HUMOR COLUMN ON A FREE NON-SUBSCRIPTION FANTASY BASEBALL SITE! If I were ever going to be murdered I would hope that the killer had a better excuse than he thought my Cy Young joke sucked. So to sum up: I was getting death threats on the plane on the way to my mother's funeral. There's no way this was worth the $25 a week[12] I was getting paid. Especially after I had just thrown away 40% of my salary on Gogo Air. Now it looked like I would need to invest the remaining $15.01 on bodyguards. At least my father looked like he was in heaven as he licked the excess peanut salt off his fingers.

---

12   Oh how I wish I were kidding.

HEY, I'M JUST GOING INTO THE CITY TO RUN SOME ERRANDS. I SHOULD BE BACK AROUND 7:30 FOR YOU TO KILL ME!

EXTREMELY FREE-RANGE CHICKEN

There were just eleven of us at the funeral on that cold, wet, dreary March morning in Amityville, New York. Stacey and her two kids had arrived from Vermont. Debbie wasn't medically cleared to fly. Nancy and Mark's wife, Ellen, couldn't get out of work obligations. There were also two cousins who lived nearby and a high school friend of Stacey's. A third cousin, Garry, showed up unshaven and in sweatpants and I'm certain the only reason he came is because he lived down the street and wanted the free post-burial meal.

I wondered if I would ultimately replicate my mother's low-attendance figure at my funeral. Because she was so alpha in the relationship with my dad, her undesirable traits were easily absorbed. As much as I hated to admit, I'd adopted some of her worst. I have a bad temper and a penchant for holding grudges. I am beyond impatient and an over-reactor. Obstinacy is in my bloodstream. My default emotion is nasty. I've spent years trying to counter these qualities, with varying degrees of success. Zoloft has helped.[13] I thought about all the traits I had inherited from my father but, whether positive or negative, it was hard to notice any because my mother's behavior constantly overpowered anything he said or did.[14]

---

13   For more details read *Hyper-Chondriac: One Man's Quest to Hurry Up and Calm Down* available on Amazon for a penny!

14   Neither my mother nor I were procrastinators or messy like my dad.

As her coffin was lowered into the ground, there was little emotion from anyone. I think my siblings and I remained astonished that my mother was the first to go. Other than my brother briefly speaking, there was little said. She was a complicated person to love, and over time it became more and more difficult to express that. For all of us.

I tossed in the few shovels of dirt I was allotted and kept an eye on any signs of breakdowns from my dad. I had only seen him cry once, when my grandmother passed away. He was seated at his desk in the unfinished part of our dingy Long Island basement holding a black and white passport-sized photo of her and weeping. But at my mother's funeral, none of us shed a tear. If he was hurting, it was internal—which wasn't surprising since he had always seemed to keep his emotions buried, whether for fear of being criticized by my mother or just because had he not submerged them they would have flooded out and drowned him in a sea of misery. I probably don't cry for the same reasons. It's easier to bottle things up and retreat into myself than to take a chance expressing sadness since my mother seemed anchored in sad. Anyway, Nancy cries enough for two people, routinely shedding tears during movie trailers and dog food commercials.

While having lunch with the other mourners at the diner, my father seemed subdued, but okay. He still had a hearty appetite and must have eaten four or five pickles from the stainless steel container that all Long Island diners are required to have on their tables. He even pulled out the eyeglass case to see if the waitress got the joke[15].

As we boarded the flight back to Florida, he reverted back to Monotone Man, a deep level of despondency returning to him. This time he didn't notice the X-ray machines, TSA agents, food court, or any of the strangers seated next to him at the gate. Now that he was no longer occupied with catching up, his future seemed to be coming back into focus. I had no idea if all the distractions had ultimately blurred my father's comprehension of what had actually happened to him.

I was about to find out.

---

15   She didn't.

TOMBSTONES OF THE FUTURE

CHAPTER 4
REBOOT

A BUCKET'S BUCKET LIST

The flight attendant put seltzer and mini-pretzels on my father's tray and smiled. My chest clenched as I wondered how awful it would be for my dad if we crashed [16]. His life would have ended on a thirty-year slump on the downside of the bell curve. There would be no second act. Actually there *would* be a second act, just a really depressing one.

---

16   Obviously it wouldn't be a good thing for me, either.

DAVE'S METHOD OF TRAVELING
WAS FLAWED

The only person in my father's life had been my mother. In Florida, he knew my sister and one next-door neighbor. He had zero friends and infinite time. His house was a mess, his body gelatinous. He hadn't been single since 1952. Kurt Vonnegut had said the two worst things in life are boredom and loneliness. Now those two things were all Dad had.

"Dad, I'll stay in Florida for as long as you want. Are you gonna be okay?"

"Of course I'll be okay," he said somewhat convincingly from his aisle seat.

"What are you going to do all day?"

"Plenty of things. Don't worry about me."

Plenty of things? I couldn't think of one.

When we landed in Ft. Myers, he seemed to be managing his emotions but I was concerned that despair would set in when we got back to his house.

The best course of action was to help my dad start some fresh routines so he wouldn't dwell on his new situation while sitting at the kitchen table or walking past my mother's now permanently empty bedroom.

I bought him an HD TV so he could watch his sports and cop shows and, after hooking it up, took him out to dinner. Still unused to his new circumstances, he continued to look at his watch every two or three minutes, unaccustomed to not having to rush... somewhere.

"Dad, what's the hurry?"

"Oh. Sorry. I forgot."

"Want a beer?"

"Nah."

"Glass of wine? I'm driving."

"No thanks."

My father never smoked and probably consumed the equivalent of one six-pack in his life. And it wasn't even a normal six-pack but those tiny eight-ounce bottles of Old Milwaukee. When I was a kid, whenever we would go to stranger's homes to check out their comic book collections he would inevitably be offered a beer. My father's reply, 100% of the time, was "No thank you. I don't drink." Which, as a ten year old, I thought meant that he didn't drink ANYTHING (water, juice, soda) and that he was a giant liar.

The morning after the funeral, I went to get some water and saw that the refrigerator was now practically empty. My father was already awake and in the middle of throwing out all the ice cream and cakes. I felt relieved that he knew he had to lose some weight. His stomach looked like he was in his third trimester and, at his age, dropping pounds would not be easy. Nevertheless, I knew food was a reliable way to get him to engage.

"Do you want to go out for lunch?"

"Not really."

"Want me to bring you back some bagels?"

"I'm not hungry."

"That's never stopped you from eating before. C'mon, let's go out and grab a sandwich."

"No thanks."

"Boston is playing the Phillies tonight," I offered. The Red Sox spring training facilities were less than three miles away. "Want me to get tickets?"

"All right," he said without a trace of conviction.

I felt like I was taking him hostage, but at least I was getting him out of the house.

IT SLOWLY DAWNED ON STAN THAT HIS
STRATEGY TO GET ON TV WAS FATALLY FLAWED

—

I found some box seats on StubHub. My father sat there dazed for the duration, as if he'd been hit repeatedly by line drives. Sure, it was spring training and the game meant nothing. But, in his current state, what *did* have meaning?

When attending Mets games we would customarily leave by the sixth or seventh inning to beat the traffic. But we were four traffic lights and six minutes away from his house. There was nothing to beat except the specter of change. Still, he became restless and we took off in the top of the fifth.

That evening at home, he split his time trekking back and forth between answering emails and surfing the internet in his office and sitting at the kitchen table leafing through the newspapers he'd missed. He seemed to look right through me when our eyes met.

"I found a bereavement class that meets tomorrow," he said.

"What? Great!" My father was interested in self-care! It was a coin-flip as to whether he would further isolate himself. I felt like shooting off fireworks but didn't because I didn't have any fireworks and it probably would have set off the smoke alarm in his house, assuming he had replaced the batteries in the past four years. There was just one problem with group therapy. My father was a master of small talk as he glided from errand to errand—chatting about the price of gas to the 7-Eleven cashier; sports with the supermarket bagger; the weather with the bagel store employee. But I'd never heard him open up about anything of substance. Not once. Now he would be expected to share his innermost feelings with a bunch of strangers.

SMALL TALK REGIONAL FINALS

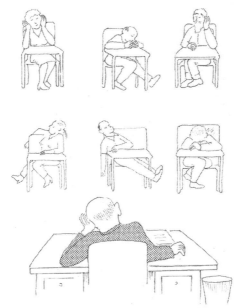

NO ONE COULD STAY AWAKE FOR
THE CAFFEINE ANONYMOUS MEETING

The bereavement group was in a large brick building filled with conference rooms. I made sure he got into the proper location and saw that there were mostly people in the seventy-eighty range, but also a few grievers who were closer to my age. I couldn't tell which situation was more tragic: losing a spouse in the middle of your life or someone you'd spent nearly sixty years with.

I waited out in the lobby, nervously wondering what my father would say when it was his turn to speak. Would he cry and be unable to complete a coherent thought? Spew nothing but small talk? Riff on whatever the person before him had said and gloss over his own situation? Or maybe he would just erupt in a frenzy of words and they'd have to cut him off like the orchestra at the Oscars when a speech exceeds the time limit?

I paced and paced and considered eavesdropping but remembered that the doors were pretty thick so the likelihood of me hearing anything was slim. An hour and a half later he emerged from the conference room.

"How'd it go?"

"Okay."

"What'd you wind up saying?"

"Nothing."

"Huh?"

"There were too many people. I never got a chance to speak."

I was furious! I felt like yanking my father's hand and marching back in there and demanding he get to unload some of his angst, like a parent scolding a little league coach for not letting his son play.

"Was it at least helpful to hear other people talk?"

"I guess."

"Do you want to try another group?"

"We'll see."

My father's spirits seemed even more crushed than when he walked in.

"Wanna stop and grab some lunch?"

"Nah."

"Bagels?" That was his go-to comfort food.

"Let's just go home."

"Are you sure you don't want me to stay a few more days, Dad? I can change my plane ticket."

"No. It's okay."

I felt guilty leaving but I also knew that I couldn't stay and coddle him. That would only delay his transition. There's an art to knowing when to go. I'm not sure I've mastered it. Most of my dinner guests haven't and often exceeded their stays.

"And you know you can call me if you need anything once I'm in L.A. and I can be back here in six hours."

"I know."

The following morning he put on his best fake-doing-well face and drove me to the airport. He wasn't saying much and when he did speak it was just repeating that he was "fine." But we both knew he wasn't. I was certain that after he dropped me at the terminal he'd be going straight to get his standard black decaf and salted bagel, hoping that those two staples would dull the pain.

BINARY STARBUCKS

For the next few weeks, my father and I spoke daily. His spirits seemed to be improving. He'd always ask me how things were going for me. Now it was my turn to lie. Going back to my routine in California wasn't easy. My marriage, my dog and my social life were all good. My work life, verging on extinction. I always answered with the go-to default word of "great" so he wouldn't worry. I'm not sure if he heard the tentative tone I consistently used but he probably sensed things were far from "great." If it weren't for Nancy's income, I'd be maxing out my credit cards to survive.

I was scrounging for freelance jobs and took anything that came my way. And I mean *anything*. A few months before my mother passed I was hired to write scripts for a reality show that was basically *American Idol* for porn stars—yes, with fully naked groups of amateur people having sex as professional adult film stars "judged" them. But after turning in my first draft I got fired for my writing being "too dirty." *Too dirty*? *For porn*? I'm sure that AT LEAST one of my bosses were aware that AT LEAST two of their judges had modeled for Fleshlight, the planet's top-selling male sex toy that's molded from a woman's body parts to resemble her specific vagina! One of the porn judges had even modeled for two additional Fleshlight designs, one of her mouth and another of her asshole. These were *porn* stars! But my Triple Penetration joke—in which I had one of the judges remark that "You have to fill out three W-9s for that"—was somehow offensive?[17]

FRED THE LANDSCAPER
GIVES HIS TWO WEEKS NOTICE

---

17   I'm sure my father is horrified reading this paragraph and now regrets telling any of his friends to buy this book.

WHY DERMATOLOGISTS
DON'T ENJOY PORN

—

PORN FOR TREES

But, now that my $25 a week death-threat column was history, I needed to figure out a way to make money. I wanted to pull my weight, not only in our household but in society. A healthy person should be working at something. Unfortunately, finding freelance work kept getting tougher and tougher as I was starting to age out of jobs. And the jobs I did get were filled with twenty-five-year-olds whose parents were often younger than me. I was now always the old guy at the office. When there was an office.

PRODUCER   PRODUCE-ER

THE POWER OF THE HYPHEN

—

IF YOU HAD A PEEPHOLE YOU WOULDN'T HAVE HAD TO OPEN THE DOOR AND TALK TO SOMEONE LIKE ME.

DOOR TO DOOR PEEPHOLE SALESMAN

Despite keeping my expenses low and having a (useless) master's degree, life was becoming a struggle. It's probably the main reason I never wanted kids. If I wasn't working, I didn't want them wandering around the house asking what daddy was doing home (again!) or thinking I was a loser. My problem was that I was always saving myself for later, putting my energies into exercising so I'd look better and younger and (hopefully) preserve my hairline as I hoarded sleep like my brother hoarded old radios. Life for me had become something in which avoiding pain was more important than finding pleasure.

THE WORLD'S WORST GUIDANCE COUNSELOR

I decided to look to the internet to solve my financial woes.

My previous attempt at viral videos was during the early days of the 'net. It was a series called "Whiny Baby" in which I wore only a giant diaper with an oversized blue safety pin and spewed two minute rants about animal rights, women's rights and religion, while squeezed into a crib on my back swatting away at a mobile. (At this point, you might again be realizing why you've never heard of me.)

But now there was an election coming up and, while drunk with Nancy at a neighbor's house, I blurted out that America needed an impartial, bipartisan robot as president. "Robot Steve!" announced the Merlot. The two people eating and drinking with me didn't seem to hate the idea so the next morning I decided to pursue it.

VOTE PYROMANIAC BOB STEVENS
FOR MAYOR!!!!

Since I'm not actually a robot, I needed a costume. I found a few cheaply made possibilities online but they all looked like something a nine-year old would wear on Halloween. I went to all the local costume shops in Hollywood, called every prop place, checked eBay and Etsy and was out of ideas. I was about to give up when I put a post up on our local Nextdoor networking website and miraculously received a response within forty-five seconds to "Call Lulu." We spoke on the phone and I sent Lulu a few ideas for prototypes, several of which my father had sketched in between doing our cartoons. She said she could do it for $450. That was a bargain! I would sell Robot Steve T-shirts, Robot Steve hats, Robot Steve key chains! They would be printed on-demand by Zazzle and I would get a couple of dollars for each one sold without having to store any inventory, mail anything or do anything—other than pushing my site. No wonder youth gets involved in the internet. It's so time- and cost- efficient. I'd also shoot videos and have an entire Robot Steve YouTube Channel and get lots of clicks, which would mean lots of advertisers and lots of money! Thank you for the amazing idea, wine!

"Let's do this!" I practically shouted to Lulu.

And Robot Steve was officially born.

CHAPTER 5
METAL MOUTH

ANTI-SOCIAL BUTTERFLY

I met Lulu in a parking lot at a fast food restaurant, she in her ancient beat-up Toyota and me in my even more ancient and beat-up Volvo, where I gave her a deposit of $200. Had a police officer witnessed this transaction and I said "No, it's not for drugs, it's for a robot costume so I can run for president," he probably would have thought I'd already taken the drugs.

While I waited for Lulu to make my costume, I checked in with my dad. We were running into some issues.

"Brian, what did you think about the last batch of cartoons?"

"The artwork is great, Dad." The artwork *was* great. The problem was, because everything was drawn by hand and no computer was involved, the captions on the bottom were breaking on odd words. Certain words and phrases just naturally belong together and if one is at the end of the first line and then the next is at the beginning of the second line it looks off. Because of my three years writing thought-bubbles and lower third captions on *Blind Date* I'm particularly fussy about this.

For instance:

UNLIKE OTHER FLAMINGOS, MARCY
NEVER SWITCHED LEGS

In a perfect world, "Marcy" would appear on the second line.

DESPITE HIS ILLNESS, CONNOR WAS STILL ABLE TO BE THE DICKISH SECOND GRADER HE'D ALWAYS BEEN

Here, the ideal layout should be squeezed onto two lines:

Despite his illness, Connor was still able to be
the dickish second grader he'd always been

And here's another one:

"Was" should join "about to become true" on the second line.

Redoing the captions would require Wite-Out which would make the finished product look less-than-professional. So it was either have my father re-do the entire cartoon or live with it. We usually lived with it. I just wanted to make sure he kept drawing and had fun. He didn't care about word breakage so it was something that only bugged me.

Nancy is equally finicky when it comes to where the words in lines break. Our 2002 wedding invitations were *Blind Date*/thought-bubble inspired.

Originally, the boy's bubble had "baby" and "we're" in the first line and "on" by itself in the second line. Nancy was furious. "Don't they get it? 'Baby' needs its own line! And you don't leave a preposition all by itself!" Nancy disputed part of the printing costs with the credit card company.[18] "This is unacceptable. This is my wedding and I'm a professional thought-bubble writer!" becoming the first human being to ever utter that sentence. She was also the first bride ever to care more about the word breakage on an invitation than her dress, the flowers and table assignments.

---

18   She won.

A week later, I drove to Lulu's workshop in a hillside garage and had a Robot Steve suit fitting. Her craftsmanship was superb. The square red head and car cup holder eyes made it look really retro and the gray torso had a series of flashing lights, as did a slinky-like arch on my skull. The gray mittens that resembled over-sized lobster claws fit like gloves. Robots AND politics?! AND a professional looking costume?! My gut was right. This was a can't-miss idea. If not a grand slam, definitely a two-run homer.

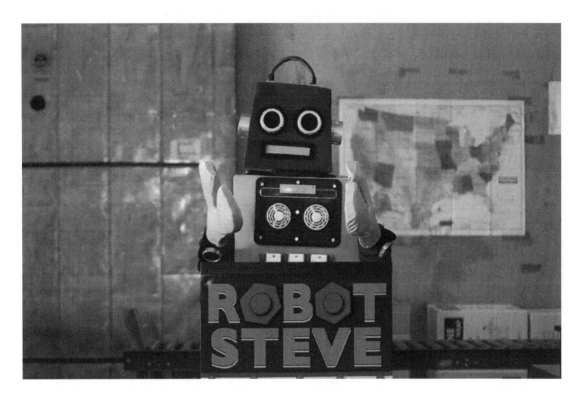

I bought a podium ($79.95) and attached some artwork ($30) on Poster Board ($18) to it that said ROBOT STEVE FOR PRESIDENT in red, white and blue. I wrote about ten or fifteen drafts of a two-page monologue—printing it out each time and reading it aloud into a tape recorder—and then sent it around to various friends until I had everyone's approval, including Nancy's.

Now I was ready to shoot my first video, officially announcing my robot candidacy for President. I hired a friend of a friend ($110) who owned a Canon 5D camera and would rent some lights ($70) so it would look way more professional than anything shot on an iPhone. I found another friend at my dog park who rented out a warehouse to a company that sold diapers for incontinent veterans and said we could shoot there.

Nancy came along and—despite the 97 degrees outside, the warehouse not being air-conditioned, the director being an hour late and one of the rented lights breaking ($100)—everything seemed to go well. Although I was now in the hole for $865.95, with the power of the internet behind me, I knew I could recoup that in a matter of hours.

I uploaded the two-minute video on YouTube and was certain it would go viral. We ordered in our favorite Thai food, opened some slightly over ten dollar wine from Trader Joe's and waited for the clicks to flood in. Instead it became an evening of optimistically staring at a computer screen with my equally optimistic wife, begging friends to click and spread the word and occasionally hitting refresh to see the number of views jump one digit. It was worse than watching the scoreboard at a soccer game.

SPIDER ANGST

After a month of hitting refresh thousands of times and hustling and networking both online and off, T-shirt sales were non-existent. Well, technically they *did* exist but only because Nancy had purchased one ($26) that said: "Robot Steve: Ironically NOT Part of the Washington Machine." I began to think that the problem was a lack of variety and that I needed a bevy of other Robot Steve products to mollify the masses. I started brainstorming on more ideas for shirts, hats and mugs... "Robot Steve: If I Ever Tell a Lie You Can Melt Me Down into Nickels" "I Believe in Robot Steve!" "Robot Steve: 300 GB of RAM! Take that, FDR!" "Robot Mt. Rushmore"—with four identical images of Robot Steve's face replacing Washington, Jefferson, Lincoln, and Teddy Roosevelt. My burst of enthusiasm came to a screeching halt when I hit refresh on Zazzle and—despite numerous friends saying that they'd "definitely" buy a shirt—the new merchandise earnings remained at three zeros separated by a superfluous decimal point that appeared to be mocking me.

Just as I was about to power down and spare my computer any more shame, I came across an ad for auditions for Politicon, a political convention being held at the Los Angeles Convention Center. It couldn't hurt to submit. I emailed in my Robot Steve video and got accepted the next day. I would be performing with nine other political comics for a prize of $500. It wasn't a ton of money but hopefully the publicity would drive people to my website, generate hits and move shirts—one of which Nancy would parade around in at the event.

The day was full of hope as Nancy and I pulled up to the underground parking structure and walked about a mile lugging the robot costume. We saw Newt Gingrich and Ann Coulter on a nearby escalator and pointed at them as if they were fish in an aquarium.

The place I'd be performing was more like an airplane hangar than a comedy room. There were various booths for assorted political groups lining the perimeter and about two hundred seats squeezed into the middle, a quarter of which were filled.

The other performers were all non-robot stand-ups delivering standard quips about Obama, Mitt Romney and John Boehner to the quartet of D-List Celebrity judges.

As the stand-up before me was wrapping up, Nancy helped me wiggle into the refrigerator box-like torso then plopped on my giant square red head and squeezed my hands into the oversized lobster claw mittens. She then flicked on the flashing lights on my chest and skull. Everything had to be done at the last second because the inside of the costume was the temperature of the sun. This robot was about to dominate!

I slowly ambled onstage—unable to look down—and approached the podium (which stagehands had just moved onstage for me). The red, white and blue "Robot Steve For President" placard we had glued to it made it look official. Since I was a robot and my mouth and lips weren't visible, the producers gave me the option of playing a tape over their sound system or delivering my lines live into a microphone on a podium. I had memorized my material, so I chose the latter.

One thing you should know that anybody who has ever known me would not dispute: Frazer men have loud voices. My father, brother, and I project with the best of them. Nonetheless, when performing in a room that could store a fleet of aircraft carriers, some electronic assistance was needed. During sound-check, the microphone worked great. Unfortunately, the stagehands now had the magical sound amplifying stick pointed straight down, well away from my robot mouth, rendering both useless. Since I was unable to use my two-pronged mitten/claw robot hands to manipulate the mic, for the next five minutes I screamed my robot lines while sweating in my expensive cardboard box. I doubt anyone but the ten people in the front row heard me. I think even the judges were too far away to have anything I said make it to their ears. Despite being anonymously hidden inside a costume, it was the longest five minutes of my life. I tried to maintain my focus and concentration since people had paid to be there. But my mind kept drifting off into the future. Because at least in the future I wouldn't be dressed as a robot.

GENE THE EXCUSE MACHINE

When my "set" was up, I plodded off the stage and didn't even wait for the winner to be announced. I knew it wouldn't be Robot Steve. And forget about potential T-shirt sales. The only mention of the shirt Nancy was wearing was from Nancy, who complained that the tag was making the back of her neck itch.

All this embarrassment for a potential $500?! I removed the costume and was tempted to leave it in the dressing room. What was wrong with me? How low had I sunk? How desperate had I become? Had I won the money, it would have barely paid for the costume and gas it took to get there. Plus I was in the hole another $20 because I forgot to get my parking validated. At this point I was just one step away from dressing up as a superhero and posing for photos with tourists on Hollywood Boulevard. And two steps from waving a giant arrow on a street corner to cajole people towards the newest sandwich shop.

Maybe it was time to give up any hopes of being paid to be creative and just look for that day job somewhere. It couldn't be any less soul crushing than what I was currently doing. Yes, in many respects I was living out my dreams, it just wasn't turning out to be a very good dream.

COUNTERFEITERS PAROLE HEARINGS

I called my father to see how he was holding up.

"Fine."

"Are you okay? You sound out of breath."

"I'm on the treadmill." I was pleasantly surprised. He had bought it years ago but within seconds it had been converted into a coat rack.

"You wanna call me back?"

"Nah. I'm only doing another half a mile or so."

"I didn't know you were exercising."

"Gotta do something. I went to another bereavement group last night."

"Wow. Good for you. How was it?"

"A lot of people crying."

"Did you cry?"

"No."

"Was it helpful to talk to people?"

"I didn't really get a chance to talk. Hopefully next time. Oh, I signed up with a book group."

"In your development?"

"Online."

"Great, Dad."

"I'm almost done with the latest cartoon. I just have to ink it in."

"Okay."

"And I dropped all of your mother's clothes off at Goodwill this morning."

"I'm proud of you."

"And a place is picking up her bed tomorrow for a hospital. I hope they don't get here too late, I'd like to go join the temple."

I was over the moon. My father's internal mechanisms hadn't changed; now that he was free to behave as he wished his protective outer shell had cracked and his natural optimism was being allowed to seep through and shine again. When it's not your time there's nothing you can do to make it happen. And when it is your time there's nothing you can do to stop it. He was ready to conquer the world. Or at least Ft. Myers. And if an eighty-year-old could redefine himself, so could I.

POSTSCRIPT:

Four days later I saw on the news that a massive fire had burned down an entire block—including the warehouse where we shot Robot Steve—causing over $2 million in damage. If that wasn't an omen for moving on, I don't know what is.

KARL MANAGED TO EXTEND HIS LAST MEAL ON DEATH ROW INDEFINITELY

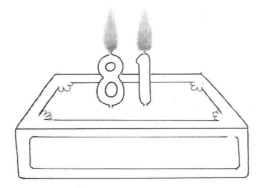

CHAPTER 6
NO PAIN, NO PAIN

Newly inspired by my father's go-get-'em attitude, I needed to get over the robot fiasco, the porn fiasco, the baseball website death threat fiasco, and the overusing the word "fiasco" fiasco. I vowed to end my parade of humiliation. I dreaded the annual trek to our accountant, Susan, and exposing my lack of income for the world, or at least the IRS, to see. I always told her, "But next year will be better! I promise!" As if Susan owned shares in me. I dreaded industry parties, where, seemingly before anyone even asked your name, they'd say, "So what do you do?" Answering, "Cartoons with my dad!" seemed lame.

THE SILENT WAR IN LARRY'S POCKET

But, in my mind, What *don't* you do? is the more relevant question. I *don't* do something I hate for eight hours a day surrounded by people I hate. I *don't* commute in stop-and-go traffic for an hour in each direction. I *don't* wake up in the morning when the alarm clock rings and say, "oh fuck!" to myself because I dread going to work. I *don't* hate my life. Just my cash flow.

Debbie was going away on vacation at the end of the following month and asked if I could come back to Ft. Myers so there'd be someone to check up on my dad. That would give me five weeks in California to get stuff done.

I realized that if our cartoons were going to go to the next level, we had to expand our base beyond Facebook so I decided to have a website built. That way we could sell original cartoons and signed prints in addition to creating custom cartoons. Although I certainly needed income, I was more keyed up for my father to have the thrill of getting checks for his craft. But I couldn't think of a name for our collaboration. Then, as I wandered around a used bookstore, I saw a copy of W. Somerset Maugham's "The Moon and Sixpence" mistakenly placed in the cooking section. This triggered thoughts of Maugham's most famous book, "The Razor's Edge," which made me think of our last name.

I called my dad to see what he thought of "The Frazer's Edge." But he wasn't picking up either phone. He never checked the answering machine to his landline and rarely answered his cell. I was worried. My mind began to race. My father had a rare blood deficiency called Factor XI—which he identified with a silver bracelet around his wrist. What if he had fainted because of that condition and hit his head on something? Or passed out while driving? What if he—in an effort to erase decades of inactivity—suffered a heart attack by over-exerting himself on the treadmill? He was also a prodigious throat clearer and always had to keep water in the cup holder in the car. What if the bottle fell onto the floor of the passenger's side and he had tried to reach for it while he was driving and got into an accident? Or, clearing his throat maniacally, he couldn't get to his water in time and choked to death? Seven calls and five hours later I finally reached him.

"Dad, where were you all day?"

"First I drove Jon to the dentist..."

Since Jon is blind and Debbie works full-time, my father is often his chauffeur. "Then I went to a book club, then yoga, then to a drawing class." It was official. My father had more energy than me. And frankly, I was a little jealous. I had recently turned fifty and still had all my hair but, despite exercising daily, was lacking in the energy department. Many of my peers were on testosterone. I'm not a big fan of taking supplements (Zoloft is the only pill I pop) but I was curious to see if my testosterone levels were abnormally low. I went to my doctor and gave blood and everything came out normal. Which is ultimately great, but left me wondering where my pep went.

"What do you think of 'The Frazer's Edge' for the name of our website?" I asked him.

"Okay." His cadence said he didn't care. I could have called it "Sam Frazer is a Horrible Human and Drug Trafficker" and he would have responded in the same manner.

The following morning, on a cloudy Los Angeles Thursday, at approximately 8:16AM, Pacific Standard Time, my parade of humiliation added a new float.

"Sorry, but I'm going to have to hire that friend of Maureen's. You just aren't good enough. I mean, the effort's there but we need to get a professional in here."

I got fired. Nancy would no longer allow me to clean our house—which I was doing pro bono.

I like to clean. I mean I *really really* like to clean. I find it cathartic. And, when we first got our house and I was busy working in offices, it made sense to hire a housekeeper. However, now that my workload was 100% from home it made no sense. Not only was it throwing away money but cleaning gave me a scrap of self-esteem and a sense of accomplishment. And if we got a maid I'd need to take my dog and disappear from the house for four or five hours. Which I hated. It made me feel like I was a transient hobo while someone was doing a job that I was certainly healthy and qualified enough to do. With the threat of potential bi-monthly cleanings, I would have two extra days a month to dread, meandering aimlessly around town, jumping from café to café, killing time as my pound mutt—animated during the first hour out and about—suddenly wondered if we had been evicted and he was once again homeless, living on the streets.

"C'mon, lady! At least let me dust!" I pleaded.

I especially loved tying up the plastic bag filled with filth from the floors, yanking it out of our kitchen garbage and tossing it into our black bin outside. It was one of the few tasks that had a distinct beginning, middle and end. Now it just had an end.

"Y'know... a lot of wives would be elated that their husband was a cleaning aficionado."

"Y'know... a lot of husbands would be elated that their wives wanted them to spend their time doing something more constructive than scrubbing a toilet."

"Y'know... Lot's wife... was turned into a pillar of salt. Which I would have happily vacuumed up!" Okay, I had nothing.

"Look, you're good but you're not good enough," Nancy continued. "And I don't want to run around pointing out problem areas and grimy spots you've missed and constantly remind you to clean better. It's not good for our marriage."

"You're wrong. It's not good for *your side* of the marriage. It's excellent and, as I've mentioned, cathartic for my side."

I'm not even sure if Nancy heard my second sentence. She was already dialing Maureen's number to track down her cleaning lady. This really sucked.

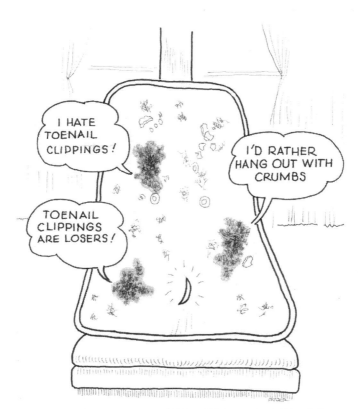

CLIQUES INSIDE THE VACUUM CLEANER

Dejected, I took a walk around the neighborhood with my dog and passed a group of kids playing a videogame at a bus stop. They had the volume up high and it was just a typical shooting game. BamBamBamBam!!! What a useless time suck. Then I thought what would happen if instead of shooting everything (which most videogames seemed to do) you "sucked" stuff? You'd suck up bugs, dirt, crustaceans, nuts, bolts, anything and everything! With a giant vacuum! If Nancy wouldn't allow me to clean our house, then damn it, I could at least clean an imaginary one on my phone.

I'd never designed a videogame. I didn't even really play them—with the exception of Ms. Pac-Man[19]. But I thought this could be the next Candy Crush. Hey, as long as it wasn't the next Robot Steve.

I called the game uSuck and texted a friend from college who had access to wealthy people to see what he thought. He liked it and was able to secure some token start-up money from an investor. My friend and I were now officially Time Suck Media with the tag line: *There's Always Time to Suck.* If it seems like I was grasping at straws, maybe I was. But I figured the more irons I had in the fire the more likely it was that something would hit. And I needed *something* to hit.

THE BEST MARKETING PLAN IN HISTORY

---

19   Blinky is a national treasure!

When my dad picked me up at the Ft. Myers airport, for the first time since the 1980s it didn't look like he'd stuffed a basketball under his shirt. He wore a baseball cap with the Superman logo on it along with a plaid short-sleeved button down collared shirt with a grimy white T-shirt underneath, baggy cargo shorts and brown socks pulled up as close to his knees as the fabric allowed.

"Dad, you look great!" Actually that was a stretch. But he looked a lot better than I thought he would.

It was the first trip I'd made to see him since my mother had passed away. He had definitely been putting on a good face in our phone conversations but as soon as I saw him I could tell it was no act.

"Yesterday I took a yoga class at the gym in the morning and another one in the evening."

Who was this guy driving me? For the past four decades his body was used solely as a vessel for errands.

"I hope you're not overdoing it."

The closest my father had previously come to an exercise facility was in 1981 when he dropped me off in the parking lot at my gym before I had my driver's license. At fourteen, to compensate for my mother's failing body, I started diligently lifting weights in our garage. Within a few years I had outgrown my equipment and needed to graduate to a professional facility. Despite being swamped with responsibility, my dad carved out the time to drop me off in Farmingdale fifteen minutes away, drive home, then return a few hours later to pick me up after my workout.

In those weightlifting days, whenever I accompanied him to a stranger's house to check out their comic book collection, the homeowner would make a remark about how in shape I looked. Then my father would reply, "Now if only he could develop his mind." That never failed to get a laugh.

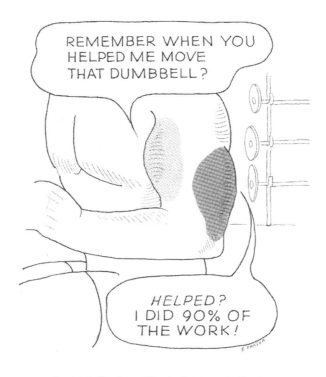

MUSCLE MEMORY

"Oh," he continued. "I also started doing Tai chi on Fridays."

"Just be careful, Dad. Remember after I won that bodybuilding contest[20] and wound up in the hospital?"

This was in 1984, and—to rid my body of every ounce of fat—I had been existing on only a couple of cans of tuna and a banana per day for the weeks leading up to the competition. Since I was still training for two-hour sessions, I felt beyond hungry.

"Of course. Too many pancakes."

"Yep. That was really stupid of me."

"You were excited."

"You say excited. I say stupid."

I went to IHOP with my trophy and gorged on three tall stacks of buttermilks. By the time I pulled into my parents' driveway, I was in so much pain my father had to rush me to the hospital, where we sat in the emergency room for hours. My stomach had shrunk so much from all the dieting that stuffing myself so quickly had caused it to expand like an airbag and almost go through my diaphragm wall. I had a hiatal hernia. The doctor ordered me to modify my diet and sleep with the head of my bed raised to prevent acid from flowing into my esophagus. We didn't get home until four in the morning and not once did my father scold or lecture me for how dumb I was to overindulge. He knew that I knew. And the pain I had created within myself was all the punishment necessary.

"Would you care to join me at Silver Sneakers for a class?"

"What kind of class?"

"Aerobics. But you don't need to wear leg warmers like Jane Fonda."

"How long is it?"

"An hour."

"How can I say 'no'?"

"Like this." My father pursed his lips and said the word "No" in slow-motion. He started laughing at his own joke before I could.

"You're gonna drive home first and change, right?"

"Nope."

"You're going to work out in that outfit?"

"Why wouldn't I?"

---

20   Mr. Natural New England. (Natural means steroid-free.)

POPEYE GETS A TRAINER

"Because you're dressed like a guy stowing away on a fishing boat."

He had no plans on changing. I could only imagine what color his grimy T-shirt would be in an hour.

We walked into an expansive well-stocked gym and entered a large room covered in mirrors.

"Hello, Sam!" said a woman in her early 70s with short red hair in tight, teal Spandex.

"Angie! This is my son, Brian. He obviously doesn't understand the dress code around here." Angie laughed and my dad beamed, proud of his quip.

Of the dozen people in class, I was the only one under seventy-five. I was told to grab a chair, several elastic bands and a pair of light dumbbells. Since I was a newbie, Angie suggested I go in the back so I could follow the others. I put my props in the last row, diagonally from my father, who was in the second row.

I had been working out for nearly 40 years and was a former competitive athlete. My father was over 80 and had been working out for all of a month. Several of the other participants looked like they wouldn't even be alive in a year. I figured this would be easy and I'd be lucky if I burned nine calories.

Angie cranked up the music, a medley of '70s and '80s disco-era tunes, and off we went. Within a minute, I seemed to be three minutes behind. One of the problems: Angie had a heavy accent that was hard to understand. Another problem: I'm not good at aerobics.

The worst part—the wall-to-wall mirrors meant everywhere I looked I was a witness to my own inadequacies. "C'mon Brian! You can do it!" Angie shouted at me. At least I think that's what she was shouting.

The sweat began to drip from my Dead Kennedys[21] T-shirt, mostly from the movement, some from embarrassment. I looked over at my father. He was kicking some serious cardiovascular ass.

The Silver Sneakers intensity was much more than I expected. We did chair exercises, yanked on elastic bands and pressed and pulled and curled light dumbbells without any breaks. I couldn't believe he came here five times a week.

Memories began to stir inside me. Despite my dad's asthma, the two of us occasionally played catch with a baseball or football in the street and he would even sometimes grab a goalie stick and camp out in front of my curbside hockey net while I took shots. But, even in his 30s and 40s, I had never seen him exert himself like this.

---

21   In hindsight, maybe not the T-shirt to wear to Silver Sneakers.

JEFFREY THE TYPE-A SNAIL

"Try to keep up with Sam, Brian!" Angie barked.

"Maybe I could if I was wearing a flannel shirt over a T-shirt," I said as I again teased my father's choice of workout gear.

"Yeah, Sam," Angie said. "You might want to invest in some proper attire."

"I usually wear a tuxedo here," my father said, laughing as he pushed himself through some chair dips. This made several of the ladies chuckle, which made my father laugh even harder. That cackle sent me back to my childhood, seeing my dad camped out in front of the television watching *Three's Company*. He would laugh hysterically at every single joke. It was as if he was in sync with the laugh track.

I began to loosen up around Angie, realizing that the only one who was judging me was me. Once I stopped micromanaging my every move and used the mirrors for guidance instead of scorn, the class became enjoyable. It began to feel more like a cocktail party with cardio.

The laughter and sweat continued to drain from our bodies, when suddenly the class ended. Could that have been an hour? Already? I looked up at the clock. It was. That was as far from a chore as imaginable.

"You did great!" Angie said as she hugged me with her taut shoulders.

"I don't know about the 'great' part but I definitely 'did.'"

In the corner, I saw my dad flirting with one of the ladies and I overheard him asking her out for "bagels and coffee." She said she'd think about it. The anniversary of her husband's death was tomorrow and she felt guilty about going out on a date, however harmless "bagels and coffee" sounded. "Perhaps I should have scaled it back to bialys and tea," he said, smiling. My father seemed unscathed by the temporary rejection.

BAD BLIND DATES

When we got back to his house, I saw that my father had another new habit. As he ate he would frantically move his feet around under the table—as if both legs had fallen asleep—because someone told him it was good for his circulation. He was now officially a gym rat, living off salads and sardines in between sketching our cartoons. It was a far cry from his decades of overeating, not exercising and basically having a death wish.

Sometimes I wish that I could give my remaining years to my father, like a Western Union transfer, so he would have more time to enjoy himself. Because, unlike me, he seemed to have the hang of life.

CHAPTER 7
THE DATING GAME

THE GUY WHO SHOULD'VE JUST SAID "COOL"

The following morning, I awoke, far more sore from the aerobics class than I expected. Even more surprising was seeing my father in semi-respectable clothes. He had on a cleanish collared shirt and was baseball-hatless—a rarity.

"Dad, why are you all dressed up?" It was a more polite way of asking *Why are you not all slobby?*

"Can you take a picture of me?"

"For what?"

"I want to join some dating sites."

Some of our friends thought he hadn't waited long enough. As far as our family was concerned, had he asked for the phone number of the woman driving the hearse it would have been totally acceptable.

Before my dad and I started collaborating it felt as if we were on a very awkward blind date for the past thirty years. Cartoons were giving us a second chance. Sometimes people get to know their father later in life but that's often because they weren't physically there. They were in prison or living in another country or another state or, rather than be a shitty parent, they'd just flown the coop. But this was different. With the exception of one night in 1998 when he stayed overnight in a hospital after a preventative carotid artery operation, I can't recall a single night that he didn't sleep in his bed at home. Although his body was there, that didn't mean he was. And I don't blame him. If I were in the same situation with Nancy and she became ill but treated me with disdain, rarely if ever showing any appreciation, I think I'd need to retreat, too. It would be the only way to preserve my sanity. Even as a healthy adult with a healthy spouse, whenever Nancy and I argue, I often shut down. Like my dad, I also have two speeds: silent and yakky.

"Dad, was there ever a line in the sand with mom? Y'know, if she did a certain thing that you'd have left her?"

"*Line* in the sand? There was an entire desert."

"So why didn't you leave?"

"Because she couldn't have survived on her own."

Most assume that domestic abuse is always a man hitting a woman, but the way my father was treated by my mother certainly met the definition. The reason he's so hesitant to use foul language in our cartoons is because it reminds him of the way she used to speak to him when she was in pain. But he remained faithful until the end. Throughout their fifty-eight years of marriage, I bet he'd never even held hands with another woman.

"Well I'm elated you're getting back out there. You need any help writing your dating profile?"

"No thanks. I'm all set."

"Are you sure you're all set? I mean this is new territory for you. Don't you want me to read it before you post?"

"No thanks. I've already gone out once with a woman from the temple."

"Great! Where'd you go?"

"We had a cup of coffee."

"Fancy! Any cake?"

"I'm not ready for cake yet."

My siblings and I were nervous at the prospects of my father's potential mingling. As with most eighty-one-year-olds who hadn't been in the dating pool since Eisenhower's first term, his skills would be rusty, or so we suspected. Debbie was concerned that someone would only date him to get at his money. (Um... money? From a retired elementary school teacher?) Mark, Stacey and I were afraid that someone would break his heart. Or that maybe *he* would break someone's heart—and not even realize it. And would he quickly become discouraged if he didn't meet anyone of consequence? Or bask in members of the opposite sex giving him a modicum of attention and not yelling at him?

His appearance was problematic. He was a good-looking man but he'd never had a reason to groom himself and, thus, his hygiene was closer to that of a sweaty possum than a person seeking intimate human companionship.

The inside of his place remained a buzz kill. Despite Debbie's cleaning forays, the filth and plastic spoons seemed to regenerate themselves as soon as she pulled out of his driveway. If he were fortunate enough to ever have a woman over to his house—unless she was a lover of crumbs—she probably wouldn't be back.[22] Basically, the guy had his work cut out for him.

22   And yes, this is coming from me, a person who just got fired from cleaning my own living room because I stunk at it.

I tried to be as encouraging as possible.

"Dad, you're lucky you're a man. Since women live longer you're a hot commodity!"

"We'll see."

"There's nothing to see. It's a fact. Men die sooner. You're gonna have plenty of suitors down here."

"As long as they're not snowbirds."

"Snowbirds?"

"The people who only spend winters here before going back up Northeast."

"But if you met a snowbird couldn't you just travel up north with her?"

"I don't want to move around and I don't want a seasonal partner."

"Fair enough! Let's get some dating photos. But I think you should keep your shirt on for them."

I took half a dozen pictures then went into his office to upload them onto his computer.

On his drafting table was a sketch of our latest cartoon, a candle on a job interview.

Then I came across something sticking out from under a pile of papers on the floor.

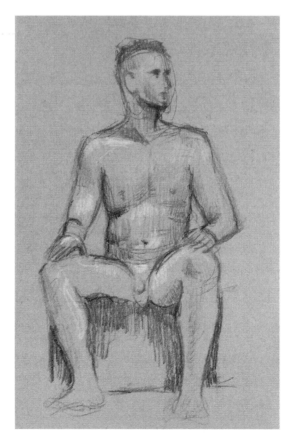

What the hell was this? Was my father gay? Would he actually be looking for men on these dating sites and that's why he didn't want me to see his profile? And if he was into men I hoped the other man was at least of legal age. This guy in the sketch looked like he could be in high school. Jesus Christ! I went back into the living room, waving the sketch around like a really kinky flag.

"Dad... w-what's this?"

"Oh. That's from class," he said as if it were a random piece of paper.

"What class?"

"Nude model drawing."

"Seriously, what class?"

"Why would I be lying about that?"

"To get attention. To shock me. There are plenty of reasons."

"Well I'm not lying."

"You mentioned a drawing class on the phone but nothing about people being nude."

"What's the difference?"

"What's the difference? Suddenly you're nonchalant about nudity."

I reminded my dad of the time we watched sports together when I was a teenager and a Budweiser commercial came on. There were a group of girls playing volleyball on the beach in bikinis and their breasts were jiggling as they were jumping around and he was so awkward for those thirty seconds it seemed like a week to me. Then, at the end of the commercial, my father turned to me and said, "I didn't know they let you bring beer on the beach."

"That's true. I didn't know. I wasn't a beer drinker or a beach person," he smiled as his eyes drifted towards the nude sketch I was still holding.

"Very funny," I said. "You've always been so awkward about... you know, sex." Maybe I was the awkward one now.

"This isn't sex. This is drawing."

"So you weren't uncomfortable sketching a naked man?"

"No, not at all. Why should I be uncomfortable?"

"Because you're staring at a naked person."

"Oh, the model was fully clothed. I just imagined him naked," he joked.

SUPER CASUAL FRIDAY

"And actually there were two naked people. They're in their mid-twenties and engaged. Wanna see that guy's fiancé?"

"Um... sure?"

"She has kind of a big ass," I said in lieu of anything clever. I felt a little less guilty about writing on the porn reality show now.

"Not really."

"And which of them did you like sketching more?"

"No preference."

Was this really my father? How had he changed so quickly?

I remember being at the mall with my dad when I was eleven. I ran out of Spencer's Gifts and proudly showed him a pin I'd just bought. It was in bright fluorescent colors and had a rhino on it with the caption, "I'M HORNY." My father flipped out.

"Y-y-you have to bring that back!" he ordered me.

"Why?"

"Because... it's... the wrong size."

My siblings and I often wondered how we had even been created.

I returned the naked couple to his office and hoped I wouldn't discover any orgy sketches.

The following morning, I showered and was on my way out to get my father his black decaf from 7-Eleven. He was in the front yard speaking to his next-door neighbor, Dan, a buff, late 50-something Tony Orlando type who was always working on his tan. He was perpetually upbeat, high-energy and insisted on helping out my father by trimming his trees without ever accepting money. He was also a self-admitted sex addict, declaring to my father he was a self-admitted sex addict while his wife was in the house nine feet away.

"Sam, I am so damned horny![23] And I can't seem to keep the older women away!"

My father giggled as if he was in the hallway at school and the principal had just walked by. I wondered if Dan had a harem of other girlfriends. Or maybe he and his wife had an open relationship? Or was Dan the ultimate bullshitter? In which case it actually steered me back to believing him because it's the bullshitters who often get the ladies. I didn't know if Dan was crazily horny or

---

23   Maybe he should be a little more discreet and pick up a rhino pin at Spencer Gifts?

just wanted to see how much he could get away with telling an eighty-one-year-old who devoured every word. If it were possible, my father would have DVR'd the entire conversation so he could re-live it over and over.

"Oh, Brian... is it okay if I go on a date tonight?"

"He's GOTTA go!" Dan chimed in. "He's gotta!"

"Of course," I said.

"You sure? She just contacted me late last night. I can postpone it until after you head back to California if you want."

"No-no-no! Go!"

"He's gotta go!" Dan was about to pop a blood vessel in his forehead.

"What will you do while I'm gone?" my dad asked.

"Don't worry about me. It's a first date. You'll be away like an hour."

"Less than that if he works fast," Dan urged as if he were a talking roofie.

"Okay," my father said triumphantly. "I'll go inside and tell her yes."

"Go get 'em tiger! Sam, you *gotta* keep me posted! You're so lucky you don't need to use protection anymore!" Dan yelled as he trimmed another shrub.

My father, laughing uncontrollably at Dan's crassness, practically floated back into the house.

I think I was more psyched for his date than he was. I briefly considered following him and sitting in an adjacent booth while wearing dark sunglasses and a fake mustache so I could see him in action. I would have to settle for seeing the expression on his face when he got back from meeting her at Applebee's, Panda Express, Denny's or—what Al's Diner was to Fonzie—the bagel shop.

"What's her name, Dad?"

"Carol."

"I'm assuming that Carol has no nose. Because you are wearing A LOT of cologne. Or whatever the hell you slathered all over you."

"I thought the bottle was a single serving," he joked.

"Seriously, Dad. You might want to shower and wash some of that stuff off. I can smell you from the driveway. And if you plan to wear those pants, at least let me iron them." They were as wrinkly as a bulldog puppy.

"That's okay."

"But it might not be okay. C'mon, either take off the pants and let me fix them or go change into a nicer pair."

"These are fine."

I was through arguing. Let him go all wrinkled. Maybe it doesn't matter to old people because *they're* wrinkled?

"How old is she?"

"I don't know."

"What do you mean, 'you don't know'? I'm sure it mentions it on her profile."

"I don't know."

"What did she do for a living?"

"I don't know."

"Where are you taking her?"

"We're meeting at the Barnes and Noble Cafe at 4:30."

"What did she like about your profile?"

"I don't know."

"What did you like about hers?"

"I'm not sure."

"Can I look at her profile?"

"I'd prefer you didn't."

"Can I look at yours?"

"Maybe another time. I better get going."

"Well, good luck and text me when you get there, please."

And my father was gone. And then ninety seconds later he was back.

"That was quick!" I said.

"I forgot my Tic Tacs."

That night I tested different levels of uSuck and caught up on emails and blasted Julian Cope music to distract myself while he was gone. But none of it worked. I couldn't stop thinking about him. I felt like a nervous Dad waiting for his son to come home from prom.

THE WORLD'S WORST MATCHMAKER

24

Here's what I imagined was happening:

My father and Carol met in the philosophy section of the bookstore. My father extended his hand for Carol to shake.

"I only go out with five-fingered hand people and lots of four-fingered hand women try to trick me by gluing on a clay pinky," he said.

"Four-fingered hand people are so devious," she chuckled in response.

Then they waited on line together. She ordered a Venti latte. He ordered thirty plastic straws.

"Better get 'em before they're banned," he kidded.

Carol laughed again, this time loud enough to disturb the woman nearby reading a Dave Barry book, who rolled her eyes because she thought Carol's laugh was disproportionate to the weak joke my dad had just told.

---

24   Although he rarely cursed, for some reason he willingly drew this cartoon, no questions asked.

Then my father paid for everything and they found a table. He pulled out the chair for Carol.

"I thought chivalry was dead," she said.

"No, it's just laying low until the trial's over," my father quipped.

Carol was a former banker. Men were always trying to use her for her money. My father didn't really care about money.

"That's wonderful!" she said as she gazed lovingly into his eyes.

They finished their coffees, then my dad bought her a hardcover of *Candide* and they walked out holding hands. Then they made out in the parking lot for ten minutes before making plans for the following night.

Things were moving fast!

"How'd it go How'd it go How'd it go?!!" I already knew the answer from his body language when he entered the house. He was slumped over a little and his usually-omnipresent smile was nowhere to be seen.

"Eh."

"You didn't like her? She didn't like you? What happened?"

"I don't think it would have mattered if I was John D. Rockefeller or Fabian."

"Well at least your references are current."

"I think a lot of these women are just looking for a free meal and have no interest in a relationship."

"You might be right but going to a Barnes and Noble Cafe is hardly a free meal. What'd she order? A three-dollar scone? That's not a very good scheme."

He wasn't in the mood for any pushback.

"Hey, can I look at your profile? Maybe you're attracting the wrong types?"

"I prefer that you don't look at it right now. Maybe in the future." He was still hedging. I felt like signing up Nancy for these sites so she could search for his name and weigh in on his bio.

"Are you okay, Dad?"

"Of course I'm okay."

"You sorry you went?"

"Not at all. You have to put yourself out there if you expect anything good to happen."

"What did you talk about?"

"Not a lot. It was very strained. Sometimes people have nothing to say."

"How long has she been a widow?"

"I don't know."

"Was she attractive?"

"She was okay."

"Most importantly, what are you gonna tell Dan? I say wait until the end of the month and then tell him that she's pregnant."

"I think I will!" he said, his smile finally returning from its hiatus.

I hated that anyone would reject my father. I think it actually bothered me more than him.

I know how tough it was to date when I was in my 30s. I loathed the repetition of repeating my life story—my likes and dislikes, where I've traveled, if I preferred college more than high school or high school more than college—over and over again. It felt like Groundhog Day—a collection of similar awkward experiences with the same women with different faces. Even at thirty I didn't want to waste any time being with the wrong person. But the thought of having to waste your remaining time searching for a life partner when you weren't even sure how much more life was left sounded like a nightmare.

Nevertheless, unloading his emotions to me seemed to be having a positive effect on his outlook. And it delighted me because my dad and I were talking about something I never thought he'd share.

CHAPTER 8
COURSE CORRECTION

A BAD TIME TO ADLIB

I was back in L.A. after what I deemed a successful visit. I was relieved to learn that my dad's enthusiasm over the phone was, in fact, genuine and translated into real life. And saying goodbye to him when he dropped me at the airport was a lot less sad than I expected. In some respects, even though I was only visiting for a week, I felt like I was again invading his space and impeding his renaissance.

Over the next few months, I took a deep dive into my projects and tried to sustain more productive habits and it seemed to be working. I had chipped away at my video game and was building an audience for our cartoons. But just as FrazersEdge.com launched, so did my father's social life. He now had an influx of new friends from the temple, exercise classes, book groups, movie groups, lunches, dinners, and field trips. For the first time, he was falling behind on our five-cartoons-a-week schedule. It was now more likely that, on any given day, we wouldn't post one.

Also, when he did have the time to draw, thanks to all his new friends and potential romantic liaisons, he now had some new rules.

- He wouldn't sketch anything that depicted God—even the standard big guy in the sky with the flowing white beard.
- He still wouldn't curse. Although we arrived at a compromise that he would use colorful language, provided that he replaced some letters with asterisks, hashtags and that upside-down V symbol that looks like a carrot.
- He wouldn't do anything political. Although Mt. Rushmore jokes were still fair game.

These new parameters were strange, as in the past he would always sketch whatever I sent him—no questions asked.

SADOMASOCHIST TREES

IF DOGS COULD TALK

IF THE CHESHIRE CAT WAS A METH ADDICT

IF FRUIT COULD SPEAK

We now also had a logo to identify our collaboration—which I would place in one of the corners of the cartoon—and a business card for my father to distribute to anyone who would still accept one.

"Brian! I've been jotting down some ideas for cartoons!"

"Great! Type 'em up and send them to me!"

Here are a handful of his pitches he sent, verbatim.

- A mime taking a selfie.
- A gorilla walking into a video store and asks the clerk, "Do you have King Kong in VHS? My DVD broke down."
- A policeman jumps on handlebars of passing cyclist and points ahead, saying, "Follow that bike."
- A lawyer in a courtroom, hands raised with a baton in one hand, says "Ladies and gentlemen of the jury, all rise and repeat after me, 'We find the defendant not guilty.'"
- A bar hopper, surrounded by beautiful women, says, "My wife thinks I'm out with the boys."

"So what'd you think?"

"I think you forgot to include the punch lines."

His feelings weren't hurt at all. He knew they were missing something.

"Oh, what about this one that I came up with at lunch... two elephants, a mother and a father elephant, are nuzzled up against a baby elephant... then the baby elephant says to his parents, 'Ma, I can pick my own nose, thank you!'"

"Dad I think those Listerine breath strips might actually be acid because that's just... terrible. I don't even get it."

Then we both started laughing hysterically at the random ineptitude of his pitch like we were two drunk guys cracking up at a limerick, as my father repeated the punch line for a second and then a third time—as if not hearing it was the problem. Sometimes there's more humor to be found in things that are so far away from being funny, they circle back around again to hilarious.

Not to be outdone, here is what happens when an artist of my limitations tries to draw a less-than-stellar idea.

Our collaboration could only work in one direction.

My dad wasn't having much luck on JDate so he joined PlentyOfFish, Widowsorwidowers.com and a collection of other dating websites so he wouldn't be looking at the same sparse set of people. Although he remained reluctant to share the details of his profile, he was more than willing to fill me in on all his dates over the phone. For the first time in decades our calls didn't feel rushed. I'd get a shot of adrenaline hearing about him out on the town—and deflated when the outcomes weren't what he wanted. Which was most of the time.

He took a date to Bahama Breeze but the conversation dragged from the moment they were seated. "She wanted someone with no thoughts who played golf," he told me. He met a woman he really liked but, after a few bites of her muffin at Starbucks, she announced, "I really can't do this yet!" and stormed off. "If the quality of one's marriage was high," my father said, "people feel that they're being disrespectful to their deceased spouse." But since the quality of his marriage was primarily quantity, my dad was more than ready to settle down with someone.

TOMMY WOULD NEVER FORGIVE THE
ELLIPSIS FOR RUINING HIS HONEYMOON

The positive to come out of all his rejection was that one of the women he was interested in at his temple (who wasn't interested in dating him, or allegedly anyone else for that matter) had become my father's best friend.

"Janice is my confidential advisor," he said.

"Well, you just told me so it's not so confidential now." He immediately allowed her to help him rewrite his online dating profile. She insisted that he "omit the caretaker part and leave out all the dark stuff." Janice may have been his first true friend since Chopsey.

Janice began to school my father on when he went too far or not far enough on his dates—when a hug isn't enough, when a kiss is too much and when holding hands is perfect. Truth be told, I have no idea if my father is having sex, was having sex, wants sex or just desires lightly brushing upper arms with somebody while watching crime documentaries on Netflix.

At Janice's suggestion, he joined the Sunshine Singles group so he could at least practice mingling. Unfortunately, a fresh set of problems arose. Women showed up, not to meet men, but to hang out and befriend other single women. My father asked someone there he had been chatting with for a half-hour out for coffee. She flipped out on him. "Coffee!?!? I DON'T DO THAT!"

"The problem with all of these groups is that there's nothing but small talk," my father told me. "Religion and politics were taboo, but so was almost everything else except for the weather and movies." He was looking for something more substantial. We discussed putting some of our cartoons on his profile so he could see if any women shared his sense of humor—assuming any of them had a sense of humor.

A BAD REASON TO GET MARRIED

Janice or no Janice, he needed some fresh tactics.

My dad decided to take a memoir writing class. He said he "wanted to do different stuff like that to broaden my horizons."

I selfishly wondered if this would cut even further into our now truncated cartoon output.

"Do you need a laptop for your class, Dad?"

"No. Computers aren't allowed. Our teacher makes us write all first drafts in longhand."

"Can I read some of your stuff?"

"Eventually."

"You sure you don't want me to get you a laptop for home? This way you can write out on the lanai if you want."

"She doesn't want us writing outside of the class."

"That's weird."

"She prefers that we store up our ideas in our heads so by the time the next class rolls around they'll be jumping out of our pens."

"Does she grade your work?"

"No. We have to read our material to the class each week and then everyone weighs in."

CARRIER PIGEONS WHO WERE ENGLISH LIT MAJORS

I had to ask him about twenty times to share one of his essays with me. This is his first piece.

SOUR PICKLES

In the Brownsville section of Brooklyn, somehow, the lure of sour pickles in the '30s, '40s and '50s, still infects my brain even today. We lived in an apartment building, which, although in the middle of the street, had a grocery store on the street level. I was always lured into the store by the enticing odor of sour pickles. They were stashed in a large barrel, and although covered, could be found in the dark. My mouth watered as I dashed to its location, as if the pickles were calling to me. I edged my small body past the perspiring phalanx of customers. Oops, my pickles were competing against the kosher salami with its heavy aroma of garlic. The salami seemed to beckon to me. Both aromas, combined with freshly baked rye bread and strident mustard created a delightful combination for my nose to savor.

I called him immediately.

"Dad, this is fantastic!"

"I'm glad you liked it."

"I really did!" I felt as proud as if he were my son who had just won a local essay contest.

My father was able to conjure up joy with something that happened to him seventy years ago. Meanwhile, I rushed through every meal, never thinking about what was actually in my mouth, just the next type of food that I could shovel in. While driving I rarely noticed the sights, sounds and surroundings. I was only concerned with where I'd park when I got to my destination. When hiking with my dog, I couldn't stop thinking about what I had to do when I got back home. Edible or non-edible, I didn't savor anything—always unsatisfied with the present and desperate to get to the future. I was like a greyhound on a track chasing a mechanical rabbit that he'd never catch.

Here I was, momentarily believing that the script had flipped and that I was now the teacher and he was the student. But nothing had changed. I printed out his pickle story and began carrying a copy in my wallet as a reminder to live in the now.

Frazers' Edge
.com

CUCUMBER WITNESS PROTECTION PROGRAM

A week later, my dad called me on his car ride home from yet another class. He now was enrolled in more courses than most college kids. "Better busy than bored," he said. Was he spreading himself too thin? On the other hand, was that even possible when it'd been decades since he had spread himself at all? In addition to the nude model drawing and writing courses, he had just started an eight-week painting course that dealt in experimenting with color. Having finally been freed from his tiny world, my father had exploded into a supernova of swirling, curious energy.

Five minutes after the first class ended, he told me that he asked out the instructor, a woman in her late 60s.

"She said no," he said nonchalantly, as if telling me the time.

"You asked her out after the *first* class?"

"Yeah."

"And she said 'no'?"

"Correct."

"And you won't feel awkward about going back for the second class?"

"No. Why should I feel awkward?"

"Because she said no."

"Who cares?"

"You won't be distracted in class?"

"Nope."

"I mean most people would've waited until after the *final* class to ask... y'know, this way if she said no, it wouldn't be awkward."

"It wasn't awkward for me. Besides, why should I wait and procrastinate if I want to do something?"

I thought *I* let rejection roll off my back. The combination of being a former stand-up and a current freelancer required that.

MARTY ALWAYS LOOKS ON THE BRIGHT SIDE

But, even on my best day, I wouldn't have been as bold as my father. He'd become Mr. Spontaneous, looking for someone to call up on a whim and grab a sandwich with.

Even though I'm 3,000 miles away, I feel like I'm sitting in the back of the classroom auditing every one of my dad's courses, his transcontinental optimism surging into me. I was more confident than ever that my video game would be a rousing success, my writing gigs would multiply and that I could convince Nancy to at least let me clean the fireplace. And all that was before I opened my wallet and re-read his Sour Pickle story.

CHAPTER 9
IRENE

Debbie called and told me. My father was seeing someone. He wouldn't use the word "girlfriend," but he had been seeing her for a few weeks. Did he want to marry her? Or at least live together? This was exciting! Nancy and I were visiting her family in Philadelphia so we arranged to stop off in Florida on the way back home.

We went straight from the airport to the strip mall parking lot of the Benihana-wannabe Japanese restaurant in Ft. Myers and waited in our rental car. Naturally, we were early. Nancy and I were always early. I'm punctual—but compared to my wife, I'm the king of dillydally. When we get an invitation for a casual cocktail party for eight o'clock, Nancy insists we get there at *exactly eight*. We're usually there by 7:55, parked several houses away, watching the clocks on our phone screens.

Frazers' **Edge**.com

CARL WAS SUMMONED TO DECIDE WHICH
OF THE APPLIANCES WAS RIGHT

This time, arriving early meant that I'd have to witness their entrance, as if they were bride and groom walking down the aisle. I would have preferred to get there late and see them already seated at the head table, vows completed.

The fact that we were meeting at a Japanese restaurant was a shock in itself. To my knowledge, my father had never eaten sushi or Japanese food of any sort. Yes, he did frequent Chinese take-out, as is mandatory for all Jews, but he was a creature of habit, and, at eighty-one, most people aren't interested in expanding their horizons. It would have been easier for me had my dad been stuck in his ways—it would have justified me being stuck in mine. My father hadn't even eaten a slice of pizza until he was well into his fifties. When he was growing up in Brooklyn, my grandparents had banned all Italian food because they believed a percentage of every dollar spent on a calzone, slice of pizza or garlic knot would be funneled back to Mussolini and then to Hitler. With no Snopes.com back then it was hard to disprove this.

My father got out of his RAV4 first, then walked around to the other side and opened the passenger door. This was the moment: I was about to meet Irene. It would be the first woman I'd ever seen my father with besides my mother.

They met when she read his brief bio in the temple newsletter and was intrigued that one of his interests was "cartooning." So she called him. Out of the blue. (Although they belonged to the same synagogue, they'd never gone to services at the same time.) I had already found her on Facebook so I at least knew what her seventy-four year-old face looked like: salt and pepper hair (mostly salt), tan, nice teeth, brown eyes, liberal with the makeup. I also knew she'd been married three times. That gave me pause. What if she was fickle and burned through men like a third base coach went through sunflower seeds? I didn't want his heart broken.

But then I did the math. Fuzzy math, but it helped. I decided that Irene was first married at twenty. That would mean each of her three relationships averaged 18 years. In another 18 years my father would be 99. If they stayed together until then, I could live with that.

A week before my trip to see him, he emailed me a poem he'd written, inspired by her.

TOUCH
something's missing
disappearing unknowingly
I barely recall it
it ignites the soul
and emboldens the flesh
lasting for a fleeting second
happening accidentally
on a crowded train
or evolving deliberately or spontaneously
into something more
relinquishing its power to time
while awaiting its next arrival
some despair
for its prolonged absence

It was the saddest and most beautiful collection of words I'd ever read. Here's a man who, after decades of deprivation and isolation, was finally getting a chance to reexperience life, meet new people and eat in a restaurant without the ticking of an internal stopwatch.

When Irene got out of the car my father's hand and hers instantly intertwined. I had never even seen my father and mother hold hands. Our family never hugged[25] or did the whole "I love you" thing. If any of us had been brave enough to drive a motorcycle, the person in the back would have immediately fallen off because he or she would've been too freaked out to wrap their arms around the driver's waist. The affection in our family was silent and invisible.

THE HOMOPHOBIC VESPA OWNER

He and Irene walked towards us, both smiling. But then I saw that she had a pronounced limp. I mean, really pronounced, like someone was walking across a parking lot with a sandal on one foot and a three-inch boot on the other.

I felt bad for her but wondered if that impairment appealed to my father. Was he just a natural born caretaker like my sister? Did he miss having someone relying on him?

I expected him to be nervous introducing Irene to me, as nervous as I was introducing Marcy Berkal—an already busty blonde with a giant smile who was

---

25   Except, of course, for Mark, who started hugging once he left the house.

way out of my league—to him when I was sixteen. But he was completely at ease as I extended my hand for her to shake. She ignored it, hugging me instead.

There was something else different about my father: He was wearing all new clothes, courtesy of Irene, who owned a small men's clothing store. In his pressed khaki Dockers and teal polo shirt he looked twenty years younger and sixty pounds thinner. Even if he hadn't lost all that weight he needed a wardrobe upgrade. His closet contained more mustard stains than hangers.

As the four of us sat adjacent to one another in front of the enormous heated grill that doubled as our table—even before the sake had arrived—I totally relaxed. It was as if Nancy and I were dining out with another couple, not with my father and his girlfriend. I think he laughed more in the first ten minutes with Irene than he had in the previous forty years combined.

"We just saw 'The Grand Budapest Hotel,'" he announced.

"What?" My father hadn't been to a movie theatre since he took me to see *Herbie Rides Again* when I was ten. And a Wes Anderson film? Damn, none of my Los Angeles friends (or me) had even seen that yet. He told us that the week before Irene had taken him to see a musical version of "The Hound of the Baskervilles" at the local playhouse. I don't think my father had ever intentionally listened to music with lyrics. Even when I was a child, on the rare occasions in the car he wasn't listening to news, he'd switch to a station that only played Muzak.

Irene was bubbly, funny, and energetic, and still worked four days a week. More important, she was helping my father catch up with civilization. Culturally, he was the human equivalent of a feral animal. She was his tour guide to make up for his decades of darkness.

As we waited for our meals, Irene needed something in my father's car so Nancy and I volunteered to get it. Irene said thanks but she'd go because she could use the exercise. Then she explained her limp. Early in the year she'd gone into the hospital for some routine tests and her upper leg had gotten infected. After further complications, she had a steel rod inserted and spent the next three months in rehab. She was uncertain whether the limp would be permanent but didn't seem overly concerned with the outcome. She just seemed happy to be here.

Before I met Nancy, I often endured romantic lulls. Then when I did meet someone, I'd project false characteristics onto the woman and trick myself into believing it was a match because it was better than the alternative—being alone. That's not what my dad was doing. I could tell. He and Irene were a great match.

"I really love that you and Sam are collaborating," she said in between sips of white wine. "Your father said you're starting to get some work from your website, too."

"Yeah, it's trickling in. We just worked on a political ad for a candidate in Mexico."

I showed her the ad on my phone.

NO PERMITAMOS
QUE EL DINERO SUCIO Y CORRUPTO,
CONTAMINE NUESTRA AGUA

"He looks like Alec Baldwin," Irene said.

"That's what I thought, too," added my dad.

The bilingual client told me a corrupt man was running for mayor and that if he won the election, he'd help his corrupt businessman friends obtain permits to mine for gold—which would destroy the town's fresh water supply. This corruption needed to be exposed before it was too late. So I pitched the Mexican contingent a few ideas and they chose the less than pithy translation of "Let Us Not Allow Dirty Money and Corruption to Contaminate Our Water."

"I think it's wonderful that you have clients." Irene seemed genuinely interested in my pseudo-career.

"Well, getting paid seems to be the tricky part." We agreed on $600, with $300 up front via PayPal.

"We only got half the money," my father interjected.

"You're lucky you even got that," Nancy said, her tiny sake glass disappearing into her tiny hand. "They're crooks."

Nancy was right. The group put up the poster on their Facebook page so they must've liked it. They just didn't feel like paying. Although they kept saying that they would.

"I told him to let it go," said my dad. "It didn't take me that long to draw."

"But I'm not really good at letting things go," I said as a giant flame nearly burned the chef's hat off.

"He's not," Nancy reminded everyone.

"Do you speak Spanish?" Irene asked.

"I don't but Google translate does. And so does my friend from high school who moved to Mexico City. So I contacted her and asked if she could help track down the bilingual man who had suddenly lost all capacity to speak or understand English. I said she could keep half of whatever she collected but she didn't care about the money, she just didn't like when people were jerks."

"Hey, watch your language!" my father joked.

WHEN PIÑATAS FIGHT BACK

Frazers' Edge.com

"So you got the rest of the money. That's amazing!" Irene said.

We didn't. In fact, it was the opposite of amazing.

"After I sent my high school friend a copy of the cartoon her voice got a little trembly. She said that that political party is really corrupt."

"So basically the corrupt people who hired you to expose the corrupt people are corrupt?" Irene connected the dots as if she were on a BBC crime drama.

Then I told my high school friend the guy's name: Jesus Chavez.

"My friend said that looking for a Jesus Chavez in Mexico would be like looking for a John Smith in America."

"So you let it go?" Irene said as she ate a newly burnt piece of chicken that singed her tongue.

"He didn't," said Nancy. Damn right, I didn't.

My former classmate finally tracked down Jesus Chavez in La Paz, Mexico where he worked at a restaurant. Since my friend is a female without an intimidating voice, she corralled a man in her office to pressure Mr. Chavez.

"Brian made up the name of a company," my father said a little too proudly, which is weird because it's perhaps the least creative thing I've come up with in my life.

"*The United States Recovery Commission*," I said, without a trace of pride.

"And *then* you got the rest of your money?" Irene asked.

"No. Kinda the opposite," I said. "They kept leaving messages at the restaurant for him but he was always on break. And then he and his corrupt political party thugs hacked into our FrazersEdge website and shut it down for days until our phone calls to his restaurant stopped."

"I was so nervous that they were going to send some gangsters up to Los Angeles that I refused to take out the garbage at night," Nancy admitted. "And I started Googling 'Kevlar vests.'"

"I had no idea single-paneled cartoons could be so dangerous," Irene said, wide-eyed and smiling.

"I'm glad Brian finally dropped it," said my relieved wife, my father nodding in agreement.

"I had to. They only owed us $300 and a used Kevlar vest on eBay cost $189.99—and doesn't protect your head. And we'd need two of them."

WHEN BANANAS GO (REALLY) BAD

The four of us laughed as Irene finished the remainder of her chardonnay and squeezed my father's hand in delight. It was the happiest I'd ever seen him.

CHAPTER 10
SH*T HAPPENS

ALWAYS MAKE SURE YOUR HIP IS BEING
REPLACED BY A HIP

The following morning I checked my email then ran exuberantly into my father's office, where he was sketching.

"Dad! A woman in Nebraska just contacted me and wants us to do a series of single-panel cartoons for manure management solutions."

"Manure?"

"I know. Not our ideal gig."

"She says that her company 'has a long history of working with livestock producers to solve manure issues.' God, I hope this isn't someone pranking me."

"I've always wanted to help solve manure issues," he said straight-faced.

"It's only $500 for the two of us to split but it's something."

"I don't really care about the money. What do I draw?"

"I'll print out the email for you."

The woman, Beth, wanted:

Three cartoons....one on odor, one on flies and one on solids (our product liquefies the solid in the bottom of a lagoon so it can be pumped out and used as fertilizer)

Black and white sketch....postcards will be 8.5 X 6....and I want the cartoon on the front of the card....with some room for copy....so almost a square....6 X 6?

We service all livestock but mostly hogs and this direct mail will go to hog producers.

Would like to use the same character in each cartoon....so we have a "theme". Maybe a pig? A piglet?

We're on it, Beth! (In hindsight, I shouldn't have trusted anyone who used four periods for an ellipsis.)

I then went to the company's website and learned:

- *The company's products are supposed to reduce odor.*
- *Since a crust is a perfect breeding ground for flies, decreasing the crust decreases the flies.*
- *A build-up of solids at the bottom of the manure system decreases storage capacity and makes pumping difficult.*
- *I'm glad this isn't my full-time job.*

My dad was psyched to draw pigs and flies.

MYRON THE SNOBBY FLY

My dad began experimenting with different art styles and using a special adhesive he had bought online from England that he would cut out into different shapes to add texture. I started brainstorming on the copy.

Over the next forty-eight hours we sent Beth a wide variety of pitches about pigs and flies and manure and waste solids and solid liquefaction, as requested.

Our pitches included:

- A slickly dressed fly waiting on a line with velvet ropes as if about to enter a nightclub... A pig bouncer stands by a large sign at the entrance that says, "EFFECTIVE IMMEDIATELY: NO MORE FLIES!"

- A pig dressed in an old-fashioned swimsuit ready to jump from a diving board into water (lagoon) with a confinement building in background. We see a sign by the water that says:

Waste Lagoon
8 feet deep
MINUS 2 feet waste solids

Pig #1: "Phil! Don't do it! Read the sign!"
Pig #2: "I would if I could read. Or do math."

Then we waited to see which ideas she wanted us to develop. And we waited some more.

"Which drawings does the manure lady want me to ink in?"

"I don't know yet. She still hasn't gotten back to me."

After not hearing from Beth for days, I followed up to see which of our ideas we should refine. She emailed back saying that she had misunderstood her boss and that he didn't want *any* cartoons. How can you misunderstand the word "cartoon"? It doesn't really have a lot of synonyms like *liar* or *immoral* or *corrupt*. Beth was full of shit. And not the really glamorous kind that liquefies the solid in the bottom of a lagoon so it can be pumped out and used as fertilizer.

I was disappointed that my father did all that work for nothing.

"Sorry, Dad. Her boss never wanted any cartoons."

"Don't get angry."

"But we did all this work."

"It doesn't matter. It was still fun."

After dispensing some disgust to Beth in Nebraska, she told me to send an invoice for whatever work we'd done and she'd see to it that we were paid. So I did and then she didn't. I waited a few more days and she pulled the "Sorry, I was really sick" card. I guess she had that rare disease where her hand was really ill so she couldn't remove the stamp from the wax paper and stick it onto the corner of an envelope.

"Let it go, Brian," my father said. "It's not worth getting upset over."

"I wish I could let it go but I can't. And this time I speak the same language as the person who's trying to rip us off. I *will* get our money!" I declared.

"It's not worth it. I'd drop it."

"I wish I were able to." I really did.

"Oh, before I forget... I won't be available to do any cartoons next month between the 4th and the 11th."

"Why?"

"Irene and I are going on a cruise."

"Are you serious?!?" My father was fearful of water and, as I said earlier, couldn't swim. (Or ride a bike. So, no triathlons. Yet.)

"Of course I'm serious."

"What do you mean, 'of course you're serious'? You've never been on a cruise before."

"Well I'm going on this one."

"And you're not scared?"

"I'll be with Irene."

"Where is the cruise going?"

"Mexico."

Great. Maybe he could try to track down Jesus Chavez for our $300.

GILLIGAN'S PENINSULA

My father had never left the country or been west of the Mississippi. Or had a passport.

"And you're not worried that you'll freak out?"

"I'll be fine."

"Have you been going to therapy or something?"

"Why would I be going to therapy?"

"To deal with these anxieties you've been carrying around for eighty years."

"Nope. I just decided I wasn't going to let that stuff bother me anymore."

It was as if my father had dragged the fear folder on his desktop into the trash and then clicked empty.

I was thirty-plus years younger. Why couldn't I get rid of some of my baggage? My fear of swimming, mice, roller coasters, raisins, champagne corks being popped and flying across the room and blinding me (as it had a boss of mine), and churches and temples should be a lot easier for me to shed, since I hadn't been saddled with them as long—although some of my quirks seem like permanent squatters that will never leave. And, as I've aged, my reaction to these fears seems to have intensified.

Ironically, as my panic about organized religion deepened, my father's spirituality had blossomed, becoming a regular at temple Friday nights and Saturday mornings.

After a lengthy lay-off, he also started painting again. I was blown away by his new work. His canvasses were far brighter and more colorful than they'd been in his previous painting stint in the 1970s. The textures were more varied and he often painted not with a brush, but with a putty knife. One expects an artist's work to evolve over the course of many decades but not when that artist hadn't produced any art at all during that period.

With my father's paintings he was the writer and performer, the conductor and musician. The ideas would flow out of his brain directly into his hand and then onto a canvas. It was like a slow-drip of instinct. There was no middle-man (me), there was no printing out an email or a Google image for reference. It was pure art.

"Is this because of Irene?"

"Not really. I've been wanting to get back into painting for a while."

"But why now? What inspired this?"

"God blesses all of us with strengths and weaknesses. I think one of my strengths is creativity. I'm just trying to fulfill my potential as a human being."

"Do you sketch out anything in advance before you paint?"

"Nope. I just make it up as I go along. Planning is one of humanity's biggest evils."

"Okay, Nietzsche. I still can't believe you have all this energy for so many activities. Would you mind if I put the paintings up on our website?"

"Not at all."

His first subject: Holocaust-themed pieces.

Hiding

Unclaimed Luggage

I've always felt an odd vulnerability as a Jew. I was weaned on pogrom and concentration camp stories by my father and grandfather. Then a few months after I was bar mitzvahed we learned that my rabbi had quit the temple and moved to Woonsocket, Rhode Island to become an Episcopalian Minister. The guy who had just spent the last three years teaching me how to be a Jew was no longer a Jew? Was this some kind of joke? I had put all my faith in my rabbi. I was actually hoping that through him God would help heal my mother's withering body. Instead, I felt nothing but betrayal. Compounding his desertion was a book he was to soon publish entitled, *The Answer to your Question is Jesus, Rabbi!* from Christ Alive! Publications.

Since my rabbi's conversion, I haven't been able to comfortably set foot in any house of worship (Christian, Buddhist, Jewish). When I do, within minutes I freak out, turn pale, get dizzy and my vision becomes blurry. The only remedy is to stagger to a bathroom so I can lie down on a cold tile floor until my senses regenerate. Whenever Nancy and I are invited to a wedding we sit in the last row and I have to either commute back and forth from bathroom to pew or just wait alone outside until the ceremony is over.

Yes, the Wedding Officiant does look like a Klansman

I only managed to make it through my own wedding by requesting that the rabbi keep it brief while Nancy dug her fingernails into my palm and I thought about baseball.

It's not that I've given up. I've tried to conquer this fear by seeing a therapist who specialized in religion. I discovered the root is that I believe that God has punished my family. He inflicted pain on my ancestors and relatives, He inflicted pain on my mother, and He mocked us with a traitorous rabbi whose words and deeds ultimately meant nothing. But my father fighting off his fears had inspired me to conquer some of mine. I had two days left in Florida and was determined to make them count.

"Dad, I want to go to temple with you on Friday night."
"Are you kidding?"
"No. I want to meet your new friends and go to services."
"That's great!"
"I hope it's great. As long as it's not another disaster."

In 2008, my brother married a Christian woman at an interfaith wedding, with a rabbi and pastor. It was my first time as a best man so I couldn't hide in the back row. I was up front and center. Before my brother could say "I do," the maid of honor started reading from the New Testament and within seconds the room began to swirl. I reached out and grabbed the closest thing to me, a wooden pole, which happened to be holding up one-fourth of the Chuppah. I nearly tore it down then wound up supine on the floor in my tuxedo. It was chaos as people rushed to see if they should call an ambulance. I lied and said it was low blood sugar and I hadn't eaten enough that day but my parents and Nancy knew the real reason. The wedding then had a brief intermission. My brother's best man was replaced by an invisible man as I sat in a pew in the back row with Nancy and ate pretzels and sipped orange juice.

THE DOCTOR WHO MAKES THINGS TOO COMPLICATED

I was hoping I wouldn't let my dad down this time. I had only a couple of days to quash thirty-seven years of religious demons.

"I hope this isn't a mistake," I confided in Nancy.

"It won't be! You can do this!"

I raced out to Barnes and Noble and got a copy of *You Are Here* by Thich Nhat Hanh. I signed up for the Headspace app and bought guided meditation sessions to relax me. I practiced deep breathing and living in the moment. I felt as if I were training for a mental marathon.

THE AGNOSTIC PRAYING MANTIS

Frazers'Edge.com

Friday night came and my father had on a blue blazer and tie.

"You still sure you want to go?" my dad reiterated. "You don't have to do this."

"Nope. I'm going! I have my deep breathing exercises in the on-deck circle of my brain if I need them."

When the four of us arrived at the Ft. Myers temple, my father and Irene introduced Nancy and me to their friends in the lobby. This felt no different than meeting people at a mall. So far so good.

"We'll sit in the back row," my father told me.

"Don't you usually sit up front?" I asked.

"Yes, but tonight is different."

"Brian, you can sit between me and Nancy." Irene was made aware of my tenuous grasp of public displays of religion.

Normally I would have insisted on sitting on the end because it would be easier to flee but I had added confidence and strength so I accepted Irene's offer.

We sat down and music started playing.

"How are you doing?" Nancy whispered.

"Fine." Maybe this would work out after all.

Then the rabbi's foot hit the bimah[26] and suddenly my brain raced into overdrive. My vision blurred, my dizziness enveloped me, my palms dripped. My panic button had been pushed. I began to distract myself. Jose Altuve was batting .369 with runners in scoring position... Adam Wainwright had a 1.67 ERA in night games... Ian Desmond was leading all shortstops in RBIs with 63... The rabbi continued his talk. *What* he was saying was innocuous; it was just *where* he was saying it. Swirls of dread and paranoia and weakness overtook all thoughts I'd sought to cling onto and I began to slink down into the wooden pew as if someone had removed my spine, my back filling with sweat. I glanced at my father but my eyes wouldn't focus on him, or anything. The entire scene was a blur. I touched Nancy's knee as if tapping out of a UFC bout. I had to get the hell out of there. Fast! She slid out and let me escape the pew as I staggered like a drunk out of the main auditorium where I collapsed in a heap in the lobby, unable to even make it to the bathroom. The low-pile carpeting didn't provide the comfort of a cold linoleum floor so I tried to get up and continue on but I couldn't. Like a dazed prizefighter, my legs were too wobbly for walking. At some point I think I remember Nancy trying to comfort me, as was a bald sixty-something man who I had just convinced I had food poisoning. I'd lasted forty-five seconds inside the temple. And that might be exaggerating. It may have been closer to thirty. I had humiliated my father in front of his friends.

I asked Nancy to rejoin my father and Irene while I waited in the lobby, hopefully soon returning to my standard neurotic self.

---

26   Google it!

After services, my father and Irene found me sitting on a wooden bench near the bathrooms. By then color had returned to my face, the balance to my body, and the rods and cones to my eyes.

"Are you okay?" my dad asked, overly concerned.

"I think so."

"When your father told me your religious issues I thought he was exaggerating," Irene interjected. "I'm sorry."

"Not as sorry as I am for ruining your night."

"You didn't ruin anything," Irene and my dad said, practically in unison.

We went into an adjacent ballroom for coffee and snacks and I was able to carry on normal, non-religious conversations with several of my father's friends as he held court at a large round table. I was still so out of it that I began to look around the room, scouting out potential girlfriends for my dad, totally forgetting he had one who was sitting right next to me.

When we got home and Nancy was asleep I went into my father's office.

"Dad, I'm so embarrassed."

"Don't be. Thank you for trying."

But how much of an effort was it really? Did I give up too easily? Were my demons that powerful or was I that fragile?

"Ever since our rabbi converted I just haven't been the same."

"It's okay. Lots of people change. Y'know that Janice converted."

"But temple means so much to you I..." my voice trailed off. I had nothing left to say.

I had to do better. I needed to prove to myself (and my father) that if he could evolve so could I.

POSTSCRIPT:

Another few weeks went by and "Manure Beth" assured us that the check would be mailed *that afternoon*. Again, nothing. I called her a week later and she said that the check had gone out on Saturday. I said we were tired of waiting and asked that she PayPal us the money. "As long as you PROMISE to tear up the check when it gets there!"

"Absolutely, Beth. Of course!"

Miraculously, the money wound up in our PayPal account later that day, but still no signs of the "check" that Beth had "mailed."

After two more checkless months passed, I was going to let her know that I had held up my end of the agreement by "tearing up the check"—which, need I remind you, never arrived because she never mailed it because there was never a check in the first place. I was about to leave Beth a voice mail of me ripping up various sheets of paper that I would say was her check and then wish her an extra shitty day. But I stopped myself before doing an unnecessarily vindictive move. Maybe people do change? Maybe it was my father's voice echoing in my head telling me not to do it? Either way, I'll take any progress I can get.

CHAPTER 11
SINK OR SWIM

CITY-RAISED SALMON

My uSuck videogame continued to run into obstacles since Apple kept updating their operating system, which meant that we had to keep updating as well. Meanwhile, my father's paintings were garnering far more interest and likes on Facebook than any cartoon we had ever put up. I wasn't the least bit jealous, in fact, I was proud that his solo artistic expression was getting attention. I picked up a few odd jobs here and there, writing a video on the history of a margarine company, some patter for a female sports host on the internet, a series of comedic videos for a health care giant to help reduce diabetes and obesity. Whatever I could to cobble together a living.

But, inspired by my father who was now driving on the highway, I decided to conquer something that had plagued both of us: swimming. Usually when I explained to someone that I couldn't swim, they assume I'm lying.

"You mean you don't *like* to swim?"

"I don't know whether I *like* to swim because I *can't* swim."

I tried to link it to something genetic, however my three siblings are adequate swimmers. At least my father had a viable excuse—his overprotective mother had never allowed him to try. But I had taken group lessons in camp. I'd taken private lessons in camp. My two closest friends in high school were lifeguards who tried to teach me. Nancy spent half our honeymoon trying to at least get me to float. Each instructor's project ended in failure and frustration.

I'd heard of a swimming program called Total Immersion. (Like learning a language but you're in water moving around and not learning a language.) So I found a local Total Immersion program and signed up for three private classes.

Frazers' Edge.com

DESPITE HIS VALOR, TED DIDN'T
DO WELL AS A LIFEGUARD

A chunky fifty-ish man in a bright yellow shirt who looked like a roadie for a cover band met me at a picnic bench outside the pool at LA Valley College.

"Hey, call me 'Coach Stu'!"

Calling anyone "coach" anything at my age seemed creepy.

"Sure!"

"So... anything traumatic happen that made you fearful of the water?"

"Not really."

"All right... Let's go across the street and start with some land exercises."

We headed over to a tall glass building and Stu led me through a series of simple movements as we stared at our reflections in the windows. The coach raised his arms over his head and told me to do the same.

"This is called 'Superman,'" he said. "Your arms need to be in the 3:30 clock position when you're in the water." This already made no sense. That would be one arm 90 degrees to your right and the other straight down. What the hell was he talking about? "And your head has to always face the bottom of the pool. If you look ahead you shift your neck and torso and you'll drag down your body."

"Got it." Assorted students and families walked past and rolled their eyes at my ineptness on land. Just wait until they saw me in the water.

"Now, this is key... your torso is your boat. It needs to be firm and rigid."

"Got it."

"Your arms and legs are your oars. They need to be relaxed."

Now I was getting confused again.

"Aren't oars firm and rigid, too?"

"In reality, yes," he confirmed. "But not when you're swimming."

We tried a few other movements that seemed simple when he did them, impossible when I did.

"When you turn your body you have three lanes of a highway: shoulder, head, shoulder." A highway in the water? Seems like he was mixing his metaphors. "All three need to be lined up."

When *aren't* they lined up? I thought to myself.

Basically, Coach Stu was trying to create new habits in my brain. The more repetition, the easier it would be to change. It's like my dad telling me how, while studying art in high school, he practiced drawing hundreds of circles and hundreds of faces until it was second nature. The bad news: I wasn't doing anything right. The good news: I was doing something.

AFTER 27 YEARS AS A SWIM COACH, GERALD
STILL HADN'T SENT A SINGLE SWIMMER
TO THE OLYMPICS

Now it was time to get wet. Uh-oh. I put on my swim cap and goggles and took off my sweatpants, revealing my tight blue, nearly knee-length bathing suit that the company had told me to purchase. I already had a bathing suit at home that I had for hot tub excursions but the Total Immersion phone lady said that wouldn't cut it. I had to get this special skin-tight suit that would reduce the pool drag and enable me to better cut through the water. I had never worn anything this tight in my life. It made Spiderman's bottoms look like cargo shorts. Maybe the whole idea behind this was to make me look and feel as uncomfortable as possible so I would be too ashamed to return to land.

I put my gym bag with my clothes, car keys, wallet, phone, and Invisalign aligners next to Coach Stu's possessions on the base of a light tower, about twenty feet away from the edge of the pool.

I tentatively walked in up to my waist. I was even more miserable than I was five seconds before. Even though it was outdoors and a 90-plus degree day, the water was freezing. This was not going well.

"You'll be fine once you move around. Go ahead and get your whole body wet."

I couldn't think of anything in the world I wanted to do less. But I needed to push my life forward and accomplish something, just as my father had. No pain, no gain. No wet, no get. So I stopped thinking and whining and analyzing and just held my breath and went under. When I came up I felt better. And Stu was right. I would be fine.

"Now we're gonna replicate the Superman land exercise in the water."

As I attempted to float, Stu supported my torso, adjusted my head, neck and arms and reiterated the importance of keeping the latter in the 3:30 position, which I still didn't understand.

"Okay, I think you got it."

No, I think *he* got it. I felt like a puppet.

"Let's put the Superman-floating exercise together with some breathing. I want you to take a big gulp of air then let it out slowly as if you're humming."

I did as I was told but didn't ration out my breath very well.

"Again."

I did it again.

"Again."

This guy wasn't messing around.

"Again."

He was like the aquatic Great Santini.

"Again."

Each time, Stu corrected me underwater, repositioning my arms and head like an Atlantis chiropractor and saying things to me that I couldn't hear because I WAS UNDER WATER!

Then he took a video of me attempting to kick and float for three breaths. (I'm assuming this was the dramatic "before" video that would be juxtaposed against the spellbinding "after" video in which I would swim an entire lap and then do that crazy mermaid flip at the wall to turn around.)

As the session continued and we faced the opposite direction of the pool, I noticed a pair of youngish kids, probably eight-year-olds, sitting on the light tower next to our stuff. It appeared that they were playing video games but what if they were playing video games with OUR PHONES?! And my uSuck prototype was on it and they stole the idea and got rich and no one would believe that it was my idea?! Okay, maybe I was being paranoid. What if those were *their* phones but as soon as we had our backs to them again, they'd go through my bag and steal my things.

"Again!" Coach Stu bleated.

What if they took my car keys and then took my Volvo on a joy ride and slammed into a tree and I was liable for their injuries?

"Again!"

What if they took my Invisalign aligners—which I'd taken out because I was worried that the chlorine would damage them? I was already on aligner number 23 of 28. Would my dentist force me to buy the entire set just to replace that stolen one? I already felt my teeth shifting back to their lopsided positions.

"Again!"

What if they took my wallet and rang up thousands of dollars of things kids want on the internet? I'd have to cancel all my cards. But I wouldn't be able to because a) I wouldn't have a phone to call Visa and Discover and MasterCard; b) I wouldn't have a car to get home to use my landline and dig up all my account numbers; and c) I'm not even sure I have my account numbers written down anywhere. What is wrong with me?! I need to keep a list of that important data somewhere! It's more essential than an earthquake emergency kit.

"Again!"

I couldn't stop thinking about those little thieves preying on the potential drowning man's possessions. When I arrived at the other end of the pool, the kids were gone.

THE GUY WHO JUST DIDN'T GET IT

At the end of our lesson, I got out of the water and sprinted to my bag. Of course, everything was there. Regardless, next session I would be sure to keep my stuff towards the center of the pool, where it would always be visible.

On the drive home I thought about how the mafia made their victims proverbially wear cement shoes before tossing them off a pier into a body of water. I didn't need the overweight footwear to lead me to the bottom of the pool. Then I thought about women who wore giant oversized earrings—and if they took one off, they'd tip over. I sent my dad an idea for over-sized jewelry that I thought could work.

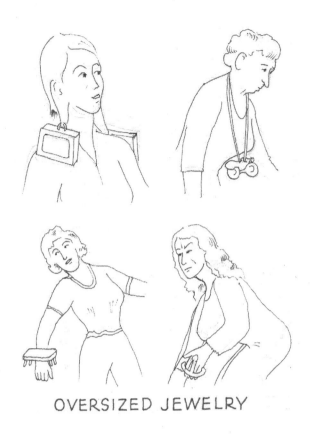

OVERSIZED JEWELRY

It didn't.

There wasn't enough room to show four different people with giant over-sized jewelry. The television set on the person in the upper left looked more like a tiny suitcase. The coffee table on the person in the lower left was way too small and looked like a watch. The scooter on the person in the upper right looked like a roller-skate and I'm not quite sure what the anchor on the person in the lower right looked like, but definitely not an anchor. So we tried it again, this time with just one person.

The items were slightly more recognizable but it still didn't translate to funny. My father agreed and that was the end of the giant over-sized jewelry era.

During the week, I went to practice in my gym's indoor pool for several twenty-minute sessions to prepare myself for the following week's lesson.

I avoided any exercise that wasn't swimming, in order to ensure that my body was loose. Apparently, I still wasn't loose enough for Coach Stu.

"Relax your shoulders!" he barked.

"My shoulders *are* relaxed." Seriously, they were.

"Relax them more then."

"That would be impossible" is what I would have liked to say. Instead I just nodded.

Those eight-year-old hooligans weren't there but there was a seventy-five-year-old man who suddenly entered our pool area. He was wearing a dark purple T-shirt as he waddled into the water like a seal. For the remainder of the class he continued pacing back and forth adjacent to us from one end of the pool to the other as if he were a prop in a carnival game. Was he a non-swimmer? Was he rehabbing an injury? And why the T-shirt? Did he shower with pants on? Hopefully he wouldn't stop mid-stride to rifle through my bag, which he was precariously close to.

Meanwhile, Coach Stu and I were finally clicking. In a series of mini-breakthroughs he showed me how to do a stroke and then I watched him both underwater and above water as he mimicked what I looked like doing it, versus what it *should* look like. He supported me with his hands and manipulated my body and turned it like a corkscrew—which made me feel as if I were about to topple over. In the past when I had attempted to swim, I always envisioned my body rigid with zero rotation. Already my perspective on what I was supposed to be doing was evolving.

My enthusiasm for water skyrocketed. I asked people at the dog park if they had a pool so I could practice. I Googled the price of installing a tiny pool in our tiny backyard. I planned on packing my swim gear next time I visited my father, as there was a pool in his development. Maybe I'd get so good that I could even teach him.

I continued to practice over the course of the week then returned for my final session with Coach Stu.

He programmed a thumb-sized yellow plastic machine, the Tempo Trainer, and inserted it behind my ear, then used the swim cap to hold it in place. Every 1.35 seconds the machine would emit a "click" which meant that I needed to perform another stroke. He reminded me to take bigger gulps of air into my lungs before submerging myself, otherwise my buoyancy would be compromised.

The sun was going down as our session went into overtime. Coach Stu continued his relentless instruction.

"Pretend that your arm is going over a '68 Volkswagen Beetle and as your hand enters the water it's grabbing for the bumper."

"Keep your eyes on the line at the bottom of the pool so your head stays straight."

"Both arms are only together in the water for a fraction of a second."

He manipulated my legs as I moved my arms. He manipulated my arms as I moved my legs.

"Again!"

He took another video of me then compared it to the one he had taken at my first lesson. The difference was startling. Although it was only for a handful of strokes, I barely recognized myself. It was far from perfect form but I could actually pass for a swimmer.

Coach held up his hand for a high-five and our palms collided.

I emerged from the water, my fingers pruney, my body sore, my mind exhausted, and toweled off in the cool night air. I felt satisfied, at least for the time being. Inspired by my father, I'd also broken through a barrier. Yes, I can still only do the crawl (no butterfly, no backstroke, no diving), albeit for about five strokes and only in water I can stand in, but it's a start. And, most importantly, my standard phrase of "I can't swim" has now been replaced by "I'm not a very good swimmer."

FISH LIFEGUARDS

CHAPTER 12
DISCOMFORT ZONE

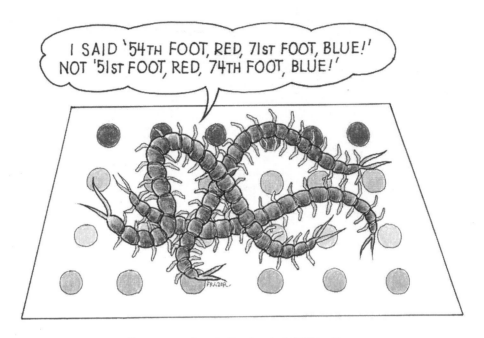

CENTIPEDE TWISTER

"Hey Dad. How's the new Aquarium Tracheotomy cartoon coming along?"

The previous version had the trach on the side of the neck instead of the Adam's apple. It wasn't working for me. It looked more like a tattoo than a hole.

"Almost done. I'll send you the sketch so far."

He had to take a picture of it with his cell phone and then text it to me because his scanner and computer were no longer communicating with each other.

Before

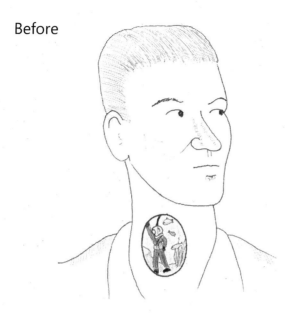

AQUARIUM TRACHEOTOMY

After

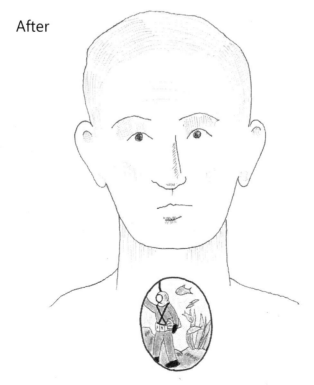

AQUARIUM TRACHEOTOMY

"Works sooo much better! Great job!"

"Thanks."

"A little bit of electrifying news from out West... I can swim! Well... sorta... maybe the better way to say it is I have a 50% less chance of drowning if I go on a cruise with you and you throw me off the ship."

"How did you do it?"

"I took this Total Immersion course because you've inspired me to confront my fears. And now I feel a little better about myself for not being able to sit in a temple as long as it takes to boil an egg."

I'd like to say that my father was proud of me for taking the proverbial plunge but in reality his focus was elsewhere.

We were still attempting to produce our cartoons on a daily basis; however, we were unable to post any because of his scanner issues. He finally called his computer guy. The problem: his computer guy usually took three or four days just to call him back, then add on another day or two to schedule a visit, and we're talking close to a week to fix anything. It's like what tech help must've been like for Lewis and Clark.

COMPUTER PROGRAMMERS
WHO ALSO WORK AT MACY'S

"Dad, why don't you find another guy?"

"It is what it is." Are you stealing Debbie's slogans now?

"But it can be *better* than what it is. There are plenty of computer people in Western Florida."

THE WORLD'S WORST COMPUTER REPAIRMAN

This was no way to run a business, the tech man's or ours. We had started to sell some original prints on our website and this would kill our momentum.[27] My father now had a backlog of cartoons to draw and the website hits were slowing down, thanks to no new material. I was on the other side of the country getting very frustrated.

"Dad, isn't this driving you crazy?"

"Not at all."

To me waiting a day was like waiting a year. To my father waiting a day was like waiting an hour.

When his procrastinating computer wizard finally did show up, he made the process exponentially more complicated. Whereas previously my dad would scan his work and then attach it to an email, he now had to perform a sequence

---

27   Actually, it was just one really rich guy from my dog park who bought two or three, but a sale is a sale.

of nine moves just to get his art into the cloud for me. And, even though he wrote down each of the new steps, there's still a technology learning curve for an eighty-two-year-old. As my father struggled for several days to figure out the new system, he remained nonchalant. I was non-nonchalant.

"I wonder if you should just find someone else to put everything back to the way you used to scan things? I mean, wouldn't that be easier on you?"

"No. This is fine. It's always good to get out of your comfort zone."

When my mother's behavior became exceedingly bad and abusive, my dad's physician gave him Effexor to help cope. But my father was no longer on any medication for anxiety. He was grateful for a new experience. I was on Zoloft and still going off the rails.

IF THE WIZARD OF OZ WERE WRITTEN BY BIG PHARMA

"Brian, you know what I've learned? Under-react to everything."

"Everything?"

"Everything. Did I tell you what happened in the supermarket parking lot the other day?"

"I don't think so."

"I came out of the Publix and there was a really angry tattooed man yelling at me."

"For what?"

"He claimed I had scraped the side of his Mustang with my car door."

"And you didn't, obviously."

"Of course I didn't. If I had I would've left a note. The paint wasn't even the same color as my car," he said calmly. "So the man is yelling at me about messing up his car."

"What did you do?"

"I said, 'I bet you want to punch me in the nose.'"

"And?"

"And he didn't say another word. Just got back into his car and drove away."

My dad had diffused the entire situation with one (albeit corny-sounding) sentence. He didn't fight anger with more anger. He'd always been a pushover with my mother's outbursts and I'd always urged him to fight back more, but he refused. And now I see why. Because it only would have made things worse and my mother even angrier.

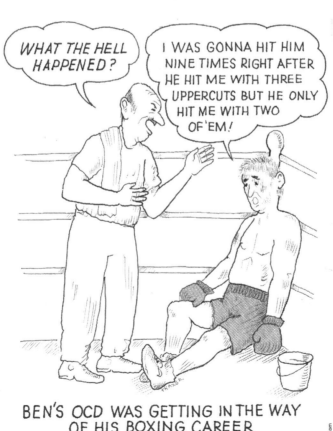

BEN'S OCD WAS GETTING IN THE WAY
OF HIS BOXING CAREER

Frazers' Edge

So, when noisy new neighbors moved into my tiny echo-y cul-de-sac, instead of adhering to my typical formula of nastiness, glaring, and being a dick to combat their dickishness, I instead began to adopt my father's mantra. I under-reacted. I pretended that the noise next door was a podcast called "Douchebags" that just happened to be on in every room in my house. Instead of my body producing rage, I internally laughed, not only at what the neighbors were saying but also at the insane decibels at which they were saying it. Under-reacting worked.[28] And it had no downside.

POSTSCRIPT:

All these thoughts about douchebags gave birth to our douchebag series.

DOUCHEBAG MENTORS

28   I briefly considered getting a tattoo (which would've been my first) of the word "under-react" on my wrist. (Which would have been *overreacting*, so I didn't.)

DOUCHEBAG MENTORS: LESSON # 2

DOUCHEBAG MENTORS: LESSON #3

DOUCHEBAG MENTORS: LESSON #4

DOUCHEBAG MENTORS: LESSON #5

DOUCHEBAG MENTORS: LESSON # 6

DOUCHEBAG MENTORS: LESSON # 7

It took a while to convince my dad of the intrinsic merits of the word, but he was finally on board.

"Is there another douchebag?" he'd ask.

"Yes. Two more douchebags."

"We're up to douchebag number seven, right?"

"Right, douchebag!"

CHAPTER 13
ALONE (PART 2)

Thanks to Irene, my father's transformation was remarkable. Not only did he have a new wardrobe but she'd encouraged him to get his dental bridge repaired (that he wasn't going to bother with), and convinced him to edit his 6,500 saved or unopened emails down to no more than thirty. When his pair of older cars took turns breaking down, at the urging of Irene, he sold them both and leased a new Corolla. To take the pressure off Debbie, Irene convinced him to get a cleaning lady. She took him to musical theater several times a month and slowly extricated him from filth, fat, and sadness. She also inspired him to paint more.

Mr. and Mrs. South

The Man in Apartment 5C

Every three months they celebrated the "anniversary" of their first date at Bahama Breeze—where they had their first meal. They went to temple together every Friday, and spring training baseball games whenever they could. On their one-year anniversary they bought each other expensive "commitment rings."

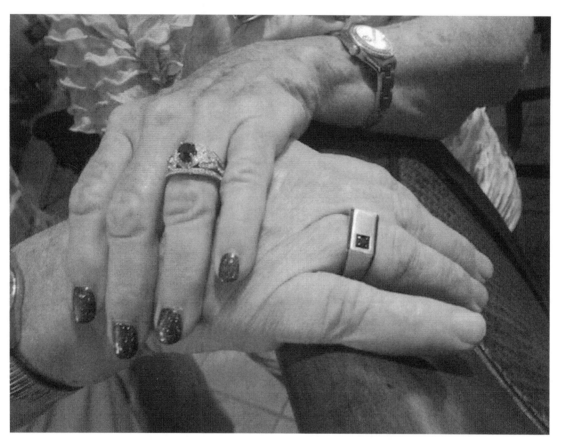

My father's hand is the one on the bottom

Irene was bold, daring, adventurous, funny. He made her laugh, drew cartoons for her and brought out her spiritual side. She was kind and generous and fiery and organized and that helped to bring out all the positive traits in my father.

Then, in early December, my dad called. For the first time in over a year, I heard stress in his voice.

Whenever my mother was ill—which was most of the time—and a new hospital stay ensued, my father was always cagey with what was really going on. We knew she was in the hospital, but we generally discovered this after she had already been there for several nights. And that's about all he'd tell anyone. Mom was in the hospital. A binary switch. Yes or no. None of us knew whether she was in critical care in the ICU or in the emergency room for a foot issue. My father would have made a lousy newspaper reporter (*who, what, where, why* and *when* was reduced to just *who* and *where*), but an amazing politician.

"Irene has to see a doctor tomorrow for some tests."

"What kind of tests? Is she okay? What happened?"

"I don't know. I will know more tomorrow."

Apparently, Irene had lost her appetite a few days before and then, while seeing a play, felt very ill and had to leave before intermission.

I called Debbie to see if she knew anything. She didn't but feared the worst. I, however, tried to remain positive about Irene's health.

Maybe they had eaten a large meal at a restaurant and on the drive to the playhouse they had an argument and she had broken up with my dad and left at intermission because she was too upset to be with him for the remainder of the play? Or maybe he had broken up with her? Although their commitment rings made that theory unlikely.

It was worse than anything imaginable. Irene had pancreatic cancer. Stage four. There is no stage one, two or three because they have no symptoms and by the time it's identified, it's too late. Way too late. According to Debbie, Irene wouldn't make it to Christmas, a scant three weeks away, and only a month after she'd celebrated a healthy, symptom-free, 75th birthday in November. Because chemo and radiation would be painful and only prolong the inevitable for a few weeks, Irene opted against them.

My father spent every minute he could with Irene, but sometimes the pain was too great for her to share—even with a loved one. He wrote poems, he held her hand, drove her to various doctors for other options but Irene already knew that her unfortunate cells had sealed her fate. By the end, the cancer had spread to her liver and kidneys and she had a series of feeding tubes in her stomach. At seventy-five she had more energy than I did. At seventy-five and five weeks she was dead.

My father had lost two companions in less than two years. Most of his adult life was comprised of watching someone suffer and now lightning had struck again. The difference was that this was supposed to be the woman he was destined to spend the rest of his life with, whereas had he spent the rest of his life with my mother, that would have been the ultimate in unhappy endings. But now the person who had injected life back into his life, who had given him a second chance, the person who was his coach and tour guide in Ft. Myers, the person who genuinely, unconditionally loved him, was gone.

It's a miracle at forty to find someone you click with. To do that at eighty-two is beyond a miracle. To do that twice post eighty seems like a fantasy. Oftentimes an elderly spouse passes away and soon after his/her mate succumbs to death, too. Coincidence? Or is the will to live simply squashed? In old age, death often seems to come with a two-for-one coupon. When you're knocked down, you're always supposed to try to get back up. But sometimes when you're down there it's easier to just crawl into a grave.

"I had bought cruise tickets for March but obviously I won't be going alone."
"Of course not."
"I'd much rather have had these fifteen months than not."
"Of course."

Here is the poem that he read at her eulogy. Here is a tissue to wipe your eyes after reading the poem.

ORDINARY/SPECTACULAR

emptiness
blackness
formless
timeless

then some vibrations
an unknown voice speaks
a brazen call from a soon-to-be-angel
my acceptance neutralized by uncertainty

Gradually glimmers of light
seeped through the darkness
soon to supplant the sun

ordinary acts endlessly occurred
receiving a cup of coffee
an everlasting kiss
a sturdy embrace
mundane exchange of words
a curled-up nose
a brief flurry of laughs
sharing a bottle of water
all of these slowly evolving into
the spectacular
distancing themselves from the ordinary
into unbounded love
Your mere presence, Irene,
will remain forever

CHAPTER 14
MOVING ON

My father met me at the airport and looked like an unkempt zombie. He wore a plaid shirt with a mustard stain—that he had probably worn yesterday and the day before that—his hair was uncombed and he smelled of cheap cologne, the lazy man's shower. I tried to make small talk but he wasn't going for that. The fifteen-minute drive felt longer than the six-hour flight I'd just taken.

Inside his house, everything had reverted back to chaos and filth. Scattered plastic spoons and 7-Eleven coffee stirrers were everywhere, the sink looked like it hadn't been cleaned in months, the floors as black as newsprint. Had a burglar broken in he would have left immediately, convinced someone had just beaten him there.

MR. LONELY

Frazers'Edge.com

It was as if every good habit Irene had helped pull out of him had been buried with her. He was back to his old ways of being introverted and monosyllabic, when he spoke at all.

"Maybe you should try another bereavement group?"

"Already have."

"And?"

"No more."

It felt like my father was giving up. He returned to his comfort-eating regimen—the refrigerator again stocked with cakes, the freezer with ice creams. He'd had enough of trying to rebuild his life. He'd already started over once, twice seemed like once too many. Not that he was going to kill himself. He just wasn't going to do anything that might intentionally extend his existence for even a second. I was devastated that his comeback was over. He had strung together several years of joy—when during his caretaking days even several hours had seemed formidable—but now he'd sentenced himself to more despair. I attempted to distract him with sports talk, political talk, small talk, but he just wanted to be left alone.

As I was attempting to create order on his kitchen table I came across a bill from a local jeweler. At first I had no idea what the large remaining balance could be for. Then I realized it was for Irene's commitment ring. My dad still had a dozen payments remaining.

NED'S HONESTY WASN'T GOOD FOR HIS JEWELRY STORE

I knew he needed a distraction and a break from the house.
"Dad, wanna go to Beef 'O' Brady's[29]?"
"Nah."
I couldn't blame him. That place had really shitty food.

---

29   Why the apostrophe before *and* after? Because they weren't sure which was grammatically correct so they just did both?

"Tommy Tomatoes?"

"Nah."

Part of me was relieved. They had shitty food, too.

Then Debbie called. Together we convinced him to go out for a meal at *The Tavern.*[30]

The first thing I noticed at dinner was an eerie quiet. Then I realized my father's feet under the table were motionless. His habit of moving them around while he ate—to aid his circulation—had been abandoned. To me, his dancing feet symbolized his joy. I missed those feet.

To make matters worse, Irene's two kids were being difficult. My father wanted to get into her apartment so he could keep a few of the pieces of art that he had made for her. But Irene's kids were making my father jump through as many hoops as possible to get his gifts back—which had zero value to them.

"Well, at least you won't have to deal with those two anymore," said Debbie.

"Yep," he answered, barely audibly.

I noticed his cell phone on the table. The number of emails—capped at thirty by Irene—had now grown back to over a thousand.

"I'm going to take you food shopping tomorrow, Dad," I said.

"I have plenty of food in the house."

"It's all garbage."

"It's fine."

"It's fine if you miss your cardiologist."

"Just throw it all out when you get home," Debbie told me.

"I'll have to toss it all in the lake. Otherwise he'll probably just eat it right out of the trash can."

"Maybe you should volunteer at a food bank, Dad," she suggested. "You might meet someone."

"Yeah, hungry people."

It was my turn to offer advice.

"I know you don't want to get tied down with a dog but what about volunteering at an animal shelter?"

"Maybe."

I didn't care what he did at this point. As long as he wasn't alone.

---

30   Also not great food but really close to his house.

When the check came, my father grabbed it. Then he took out his reading glasses to see the amount, leaving his eyeglass case on the table's edge. When the waitress came by to pick up his credit card she glanced at the case and saw the eye exam cartoon and chuckled. That seemed to ignite my father's spirits.

"Most people don't get that." It was the longest string of words he had spoken at dinner.

"Well, most people are stupid," replied the waitress.

My father and she shared a smile. It was the highlight of the night. His feet may have even moved a bit under the table.

Frazers' Edge.com

I was exhausted from jet lag and went to bed early. When I got up to go to the bathroom in the middle of the night I saw the light on in my father's office. He was at his drawing table sketching out a horse gluing on a unicorn's horn. Some of the despair from his face had finally lifted. His eyes briefly acknowledged my presence and then shifted back to his drawing table.

If time didn't heal all wounds then maybe art could.

HOW HORSES AVOID PAYING TAXES

—

CHAPTER 15
SCAM SAM

THE GUY WHO DIDN'T GET IT

With all the excess time on his hands without Irene, my father began churning out cartoons. Of course, I would've much rather he never did another cartoon and have him happy. But at least that kept him occupied.

Nancy was putting in long hours at work and since I went to sleep so early—and was usually up by 5:45 to start my day—we rarely saw each other. The frustration of not getting a steady paycheck, or any paycheck (for that matter) was starting to get to me. Again. Because frustration seems to come in waves.

In the meantime, I started making some commercials for uSuck. However, with only one programmer on the job and the constant additional work we had to do for Apple, the actual game still wasn't ready for release.

I tried to buy rights to using "Weird Al" Yankovic's "Sports Song" which contained the lyrics,

We're great (We're great)
And you suck (You suck)
We're great (We're great)
And you suck (You suck)
We're great (We're great)
And you suck (You suck)
You see there's us (We're great)
And then there's you (You suck)
We're really, really great (Really great)
In contrast, you really suck (Really suck)
Okay, full disclosure, we're not that great
But nevertheless, you suck

The plan was to put up some banner ads on specific sites and tailor our sucky slogans to each.

For instance:

- ON A GAMER SITE: "At least 83% suckier than whatever you're playing now."
- ON A KID'S SITE: "uSuck: It sounds dirty but it's totally clean!"
- ON INSTAGRAM: "Suck it and see!"

Incidentally, here's the reason I don't get more in-depth about the game. This is a typical text from our programmer.

OK updated spline mesh path mover code totally rewritten under new specs and as a bonus it now follows the NavMesh of the objects really tightly. So now that I have it all done, I need to remake the paths in the other levels, not hard but we take me a few more hours after dinner, the only thing I actually have to recreate is the physical spline path in the level for each object that requires one.

I think the only word I understood is "updated."

The prospects for uSuck seemed non-sucky so I shared my optimism with my dad, not exactly the target-audience for a video game. On the other hand, I wasn't in our target audience either.

"Brian, I think I'm almost ready to get back out there." It had been about a month since Irene had died.

"Great! Online?"

"No. Someone told me about 'Moving On' meetings."

These were less "dating" and more gatherings of widowed seniors snacking and schmoozing.

"Excellent! I'm sure you'll be a huge hit there."

"Now that I think about it, it may be too soon."

"It's never too soon when you're eighty-three! Irene would totally approve. I mean, if the situations were reversed wouldn't you feel okay about Irene getting back out there?"

"I guess."

That night my father drove thirty-five minutes to the lounge of a hotel to meet potential soul mates.

"It was a disaster."

"What happened?"

"Hollow conversations happened. I actually found the whole experience depressing."

My father was moving on from "Moving On."

"What about going back online?"

"It's the same people."

"I'm sure there's some fresh blood. Lucky for you, husbands are always dying. Try some different sites."

"I'll have to think about it."

SUPER SPECIALIZED DATING SERVICES

With some long-distance pestering he finally resumed his internet dating search and met Pam, a perky 70-year-old brunette who could pass for 60. Because my father isn't great at asking questions for fear of "prying," even after a month of dating he still had no idea what Pam did for a living or anything about her prior relationships or marriages. She was allegedly an author of children's books but no further details emerged. Not only was Pam attractive but my father told me she was very affectionate, as were her two Saint Bernards. He loves dogs, especially large ones—hence the three Old English Sheepdogs when I was growing up. He was in paradise.

Pam set up a little art studio for my father to do our cartoons, as the Saint Bernards looked on approvingly.

The second St. Bernard is taking the photo

For the next few weeks my dad and I focused exclusively on dog cartoons.

WHY GARY NEVER WON THE IDITAROD

IF PEOPLE WERE EXACTLY LIKE DOGS

Before long he was staying at Pam's more than at his house, which she, oddly, had no interest in visiting. He also paid for every meal, every movie, every everything. A dollar never left her purse.

Out of the blue, Pam informed my father that she wanted to do stand-up in a comedy team with me despite a) never having met me; b) never having done stand-up; and c) me having zero interest in going back to stand-up. There was definitely something wrong with Pam.

Then, just when my father was completely addicted to this new lifestyle with her, Pam pulled the plug. Suddenly she had no room in her schedule for him. Allegedly, all of her spare time was being sucked up by her "grant writing"— applying to various organizations so she could get money for her "educational" projects. Instead of seeing each other three or four times a week, it was down to once every two weeks, at best. And she never answered the phone when he called so all communication was one-way on her terms, text and email only. It seemed obvious to me that she was seeing other men on the side. My father, still a relative dating novice, didn't suspect anything, but was getting frustrated—he still loved spending time with her when she occasionally tossed out a scrap of a few hours.

"Dad, you can't put all your eggs in the Pam basket. You need to start looking for other people."

"I don't work that way."

"Well then cut her loose and start looking. Has Debbie finally met her?"

"No."

"That's another red flag. She knows we're onto her game."

Whenever Debbie had plans to meet her, Pam made excuses to get out of it at the last second. In fact, despite living just five miles away, Pam repeatedly dodged Debbie's attempts to get together. Pam's manipulative passive/aggressive behavior was making me hate her—which, I told my father and which, for some odd reason, he relayed to Pam.

"Why did you tell Pam that I hated her?" I don't know why I cared that she knew what I thought of her but part of me felt guilty.

"I don't know. I just did."

"Well, that's not exactly going to endear her to you and make her want to spend more time with you. Sometimes when I tell you things it's just for you."

BOBBY AND DENISE'S DAYS
WERE NUMBERED

Frazers' Edge.com

Pam was bad news. I knew it, my siblings knew it, Nancy knew it, people at the dog park knew it and, I suspect, even Pam knew it. The only person in denial was my father.

"She's using you, Dad! Can't you see it?"

"She's not using me. She's just really busy."

"We're both right. She's busy using you."

My concerns fell on deaf ears. The tension between my dad and me became palpable. I didn't know what to do. Then Pam made her move. I didn't have to do anything.

"Sam, I'm so sorry that we haven't been able to spend as much time together as I'd like," she told him via a text.

"Me too," he texted back.

"But this grant writing is taking up all of my time."

"Yes, I know."

"But... if I *had* the actual grant money I was applying for then I wouldn't have to write all these grants and I'd have more time—a LOT more time—to spend with you."

"What sort of money?"

"The one I've been working on is for $7,840. If you wrote me out a check today, we could have dinner tomorrow."

My father contemplated writing out a small check of $50 or $100.

"Dad, are you nuts!? So if you give her $200 do you get to spend twice as much time with her as if you doled out $100? Are you dating a parking meter?"

After pleading with my father not to give Pam any money, he didn't. And she stopped contacting him. Even though my hunch about her was correct, I would've much rather been wrong and not had my father back out on the singles circuit. But there he was again. At least the frustrations of waiting for the phone to ping at the age of 83 had ended. Who can put up with that nonsense at his age? Actually, at any age.

"Dad, you're better off without her."

"I know," he said. But he didn't believe it.

JASPER'S MONEY SAVING TIPS

CHAPTER 16
BRICK WALLS

EMPLOYEES AT THE "NO TRESPASSING" SIGN FACTORY
OFTEN WENT HOME BEFORE EVEN STARTING WORK

Pam-less, my father sunk his energies back into our cartoons. Although, still reeling from the breakup, he had trouble concentrating and wasn't producing his best work.

The caption: LOU COULD NEVER DECIDE WHETHER TO SIT AT A TABLE OR THE COUNTER

Attempt #1: It looks like a giant piece of licorice. It's supposed to be a really long straw.

LOU COULD NEVER DECIDE WHETHER TO SIT AT A TABLE OR THE COUNTER

Attempt #2: Now it looks like the guy just has a really long tongue.

LOU COULD NEVER DECIDE WHETHER TO SIT AT
A TABLE OR THE COUNTER

Attempt #3: Now it looks like a peppermint stick.

LOU COULD NEVER DECIDE WHETHER TO SIT AT
A TABLE OR THE COUNTER

Attempt #4: Not perfect, but you can sort of tell it's a giant straw now.

No matter how much he insisted "everything was okay" I felt his sadness. He was beginning to lose faith that he would ever meet anyone again.

I wanted to send Pam a series of checks for odd amounts, all under a dollar. Thirty-seven cents, four cents, nineteen cents, each with a different message written in the lower left hand corner memo, such as "My dad hates you," "Good luck with your next scam," and "Even though this is a nickel, I bet you a dime you'll still cash it!"[31] But I didn't. If I'm not going to yell at the douchebags in my cul-de-sac or seek revenge on people who renege on my manure work, I'm not going to antagonize an elderly crazy dog lady in Florida.

In the scrum of writing and testing uSuck levels, I got a mass email from a friend promoting her local comedy show. For whatever reason—perhaps inspired by Pam's bizarre "comedy team" desire—I decided to seek a spot after an eighteen-and-a-half-year hiatus. Between the mid-'80s and mid-'90s I had done two hundred shows a year but I had been on stage exactly zero times since "retiring." I wasn't doing it for the money because there was no more money in stand-up unless you were willing to travel. A lot. Maybe part of it was so Nancy could finally see me perform since I had quit stand-up a few years before we'd met. Or maybe it was just to prove to Nancy that I wasn't useless. I had major marriage guilt for not contributing more to the household besides loading[32] the dishwasher and walking our dog. Best-case scenario: I could see if I had any regrets about no longer performing. Worst case scenario: It would be a debacle and I would regret going back out there.

---

31   Which would have had to be written very small.

32   And unloading!

OPEN MIC NIGHT IN YOUR GARDEN

RACCOON OPEN MIC NIGHT

The world had changed immeasurably since my last stand-up appearance in the previous century. Now everyone had cell phones pointed at the stage and could post snippets of your act on Instagram, Facebook, Snapchat, Twitter, Charonch or Splooky[33] without permission. At least 5% of any given audience seemed to leave their ringers on and twice that number never made eye contact with the stage—they were too busy texting. Today's stand-ups were competing with the entire internet for the audience's attention. It was a whole new ballgame.

THE LATEST TECHNOLOGY
Frazers' Edge.com

The last time my father had seen me perform I was the headliner at *Catch a Rising Star* in Princeton, New Jersey. Because of his highway fear, in order to get there from his house he had to drive 15 minutes to the Long Island Railroad, take a 45-minute train into Manhattan, switch trains, and take an Amtrak for

---

33   My attempt at predicting names of future social media groups so the book doesn't seem dated in five years.

another 45 minutes, then take a cab for 10 minutes to the hotel/club to meet his cousin, Helene, who lived in Jersey.

Whenever I invited anyone I knew to come and see me it was always carefully calculated. *Catch* was one of the best rooms in the country. Thursday nights were usually rocking and the other acts that were going on before me were clean, non-aggressive and didn't use props. Unfortunately, all of my due diligence didn't account for that evening being closed off for a private party, the two worst words a comic can hear besides "armed heckler." The reason private parties are so horrible is that nobody there is interested in hearing any material. All they want you to do is shit on Hal from Human Resources or Betty in Accounting. That's not what I do. I had to do fifty minutes for these clowns and they ate me alive. It's tough to compete with a room full of loud people who all know each other and are drunkenly shouting at one another. Plus, because there were no outside paying customers, there was nobody to complain about the zoo-like conditions. I was stuck with this.

I glanced at my watch after suffering through what I assumed was at least half of the time I was contracted to do. Um. Nope. I had done exactly six minutes. Six. I had to endure this madness for another forty-four minutes while my father and cousin saw me getting my ass handed to me. Even worse, I would then have to face them after the show. It was a lifetime of humiliation crammed into less than an hour. My father seemed to understand the vile conditions but it must've been even harder for him to watch than it was for me to stand up there. After I got off stage I wanted to crawl into a hole. My dad had traveled over two hours in each direction to see *this*? Fortunately he was always in a rush to get back home to my mother so our post-show conversation would be brief regardless of how good or bad things went. It was basically me saying "Sorry it was so awful to watch and thanks for coming" and him responding, "Speak to you tomorrow." Thinking back on that night, it made me reconsider whether I wanted to open that stand-up can of worms again.

But, with Nancy's encouragement, I decided to mount this mini-comeback.

Because I tended not to write topical material, I had plenty of archived bits to choose from to form a nucleus of a set. I was scheduled for twelve minutes and decided to mix together the old and the new. For some of my "new" stuff, I was able to take our cartoons and translate them into oral material.

For example:

KYLE, THE BLABBERMOUTH MIME

On stage I just sang the words, "Kyle, the Blabbermouth Mime," as if it were a Saturday morning kids' show jingle. I then did a series of slow, plodding stock mime moves—trapped in a box, pulling a rope, etc. After another long beat I turned into the microphone and quietly said, "Hey." And that was that.

WHO'S TECHNICALLY ANGRIER?

For the above cartoon to work verbally I had to insert specific names to frame the joke quickly. "If Peter Dinklage said, 'I've had it up to here...'" I said as I put my hand parallel to the ground and raised it to the top of my head. "Is he more pissed off than if LeBron James said, 'I've had it up to here?'" I asked, now aiming my hand towards my waist.

THE WORLD'S WORST SECRET AGENT

Frazers' Edge .com

This one I converted into a "quick impression." "Quick impression: The world's worst secret agent. This is my impression of the *worst* secret agent in the world." Then I angled my body to the right and said, very over-dramatically, "Excuse me, sir. How much is the Snickers Bar?" I then angled my body to the left (to distinguish between the two radically different characters I was portraying) and answered, "79 cents." Then I turned back to the right to again become the first character and really really over-the-top, practically winking, yelled the words, "Oh. Is there a SECRET AGENTS' DISCOUNT?!"

The one below was more like a standard comic doing observational material.

WHAT HAPPENS IF YOU DON'T HAVE A REAL ESTATE LICENSE

"Why do you need a license to show real estate? Seriously. What's the worst thing that could possibly happen? 'And on your left is the kitchen... oh shit! That's the bedroom! Run! I don't have a license!!!!'"

All the performers received the same amount: Twenty bucks (cash!) and all the pizza we wanted—which for me was about $35 worth. Although I was rusty, I also felt good up there, as if spending some time with an old friend. On the other hand, I wasn't sure that I wanted to see that friend on a regular basis. Nancy enjoyed seeing me perform and encouraged me to look for more stage time. I told her I would think about it.

That was the same response my father was getting whenever he asked someone out.

"Can we hold hands?"

"I'm gonna have to think about it."

He was finally online dating again in addition to asking out people in parking lots, bagel stores, tai chi classes and car dealerships. I was over the moon.

"Dad, what made you get back out there?"

"I have limited time left."

He was ready. Unfortunately, nobody else was.

I felt like paying someone to date him just so he wouldn't be alone.

He went on five dates with a grandmother from Indiana who refused all physical contact. When my dad finally questioned her behavior she simply said she "wasn't the hugging type. I have to work on that." You're 86, lady! How much more time do you need? My father had developed into a hugger at 80 so anything was possible.

Sometimes my father would slip up and be a little too brash in his approach. He told a woman at a book group, "Excuse me, but your lips look lonely." Even discussing that incident on the phone with him the other day still embarrassed us both.

I was under the weather and figured it was the flu. I saw my regular doctor, who prescribed Tamiflu.[34] After taking the recommended dosage, I instantly felt worse—as if the medication were the antidote to life. Instead of allowing me to rest, it just made me super hyper and I began pacing in my living room. If I were wearing a Fitbit I probably would have made my daily step quota within an hour. I was like a tiger trapped in a cage. Then Nancy headed out and I suddenly felt lonely. "Where is she? Is today Saturday when she does tap-dancing in Silver Lake for three and a half hours? No, it's Friday. I mean, I think it's Friday. Maybe it's Tuesday. But it's definitely not Saturday. Where the hell is she?! And why would she choose RIGHT NOW to disappear when I needed her more than ever? Hey, maybe she just took the dog on a really long hike? Nope. The dog is right here. What's going on?"

I looked at my watch and thought she had been gone two or three hours. It had been two minutes. Time had essentially stopped for me.

---

34   Hey! I was right!

I had never felt this disconnected to myself in my life. I continued to pace back and forth, back and forth, wearing out a path in our area rug, waiting for time to pass so I would feel better but the seconds felt like hours and the hours felt like months. The flu was now the least of my problems.

It was as if a stranger had broken into my body and duct-taped the actual me to a radiator. I had no idea what was happening, but I needed it to end soon. I was having a major breakdown. I was unable to walk the dog. I was unable to do anything, even send an email. And where the fuck was Nancy?!?! (She had now been gone all of four minutes.) I began crying. And I'm not a crier. The last time I had cried was at least twenty-five years prior after injuring my back squatting. In between the tears, I was too restless to even consider a nap.

Nancy came home—she had been at the corner market buying bananas and coconut water—and didn't know what to do so she got my doctor on the phone. After they spoke for a while, it was my turn. My physician asked me if I was suicidal. What an insulting question! I couldn't handle this battle with time I was in and I wanted to walk into traffic. I wanted to leap off a building. I wanted to end it all so I could escape this self-imprisonment.

I answered, matter-of-factly, "Yes."

Little advice: don't use the "S" word unless you really mean it.

NOBODY TOOK POSSUM SUICIDE NOTES SERIOUSLY

A few hours later (at least I think it was hours—it could have been ten seconds or three weeks) there was a knock at our front door. A pair of police officers asked me my name and then handcuffed me. What was going on?!? I hadn't broken any laws—unless Nancy had called the police because I'd started to clean the bathroom again. I was not only concerned about where they were taking me (and why!) but whether the neighbors would think that I hit Nancy. I mean, why else do cops show up at a childless married couple's house besides domestic violence? The icing on the cake was that their squad car was parked in the middle of our cul-de-sac blocking all the other residents—including the douchebags—from coming or going so I felt responsible for that, too.

Not only was I innocent of any possible crime, these overzealous jerk-offs had put the handcuffs on me too tight so I was losing circulation in my fingers. This wasn't exactly making me not want to kill myself. About the only argument for life right now was that my father had finally rediscovered happiness and my death would destroy all he had been accruing as well as dilute any of his future happiness.

"Where are you taking him?" Nancy was equally perplexed. "He didn't do anything!" Even if the flu disappeared from my body instantly, this was the single worst day of my life.

My thoughts continued to race, too quickly for my brain to catch up. It didn't take much to connect the dots. Handcuffs inside equals sex. Handcuffs outside equals jail. Or prison. I didn't really know the difference between the two under the best of mental circumstances. And time was already moving so slowly that even a menial sentence—for what, I still didn't know—would seem like eternity. Also, crying isn't ideal behavior when you're meeting a brand-new person in a prison cell. Or jail cell. I still don't know the difference.

After another five minutes of my driveway captivity, Nancy got to the bottom of it. Apparently, in California a person with mental illness can be detained against their will for a psychiatric hospitalization for up to 72 hours. It was called a 5150. I was now technically a lunatic.

Nancy begged and pleaded and was able to convince the police that she could handle things from there and miraculously they agreed and left. Then they came back because they had forgotten to remove my handcuffs. But I still had an obstacle course of shame ahead of me.

Nancy rushed me to urgent care where I was given some Xanax to (hopefully) calm me down. The doctor told me it was *probably* the Tamiflu but that I should make an appointment with a psychologist, "just in case it wasn't."

We went home and began calling every psychologist in town. The earliest any could see me was in three weeks. I had no idea if I'd be alive in three weeks. I was still suicidal, albeit not-as-determined to kill myself as before. More like suicide-lite.

LYLE'S TIME SAVERS

Finally, Nancy found a psychologist who could squeeze me in immediately. He was a middle-aged Asian man with an extra calm demeanor who spoke with me for an hour. He didn't think I needed any special meds or something to replace my Zoloft—the only medication I was taking. He did suggest making a therapist appointment—accompanied by Nancy since I was still too fragile, delirious and restless to be alone.

I revisited the Headspace meditation app and tried to practice my breathing and calm down, but it just made me cry more.

Meanwhile, Nancy was starting a new job in a week and if I didn't recover before then, I couldn't fathom surviving. She was scared to leave me alone in the house. Even scarier—I was still frightened to be alone. Throughout my life, I've loved my solitude. But now the thought of being by myself for fifteen seconds petrified me.

In between crying and binge-watching episodes of "Rick and Morty," I began doing research on Tamiflu. I was relieved when I learned that it wasn't me at all. It was the damn medication. "Some of Tamiflu's potentially serious side effects include delusions, hallucinations, suicidal thoughts and psychosis." Yep. I had all four of those. In fact, I soon learned that "Japan had banned Tamiflu after eighteen fatalities linked to the drug in seventeen months." A Japanese teenager jumped eleven stories to his death while on the drug. Two weeks before that a fourteen-year-old girl jumped to her death. A seventeen-year-old boy took Tamiflu, walked out of his house and stood in front of an oncoming truck. *While smiling.*

Whenever you hear the rapid-speak listy ramblings at the end of every pharmaceutical commercial you gloss over all of the "may cause side-effects" crammed into the last three seconds. Well, it looked like I was the "may cause" guy it applied to.

[FYI: On average, experts say that Tamiflu shortens the time you're sick by about ONE DAY. And potentially shortens the time you're alive by decades.]

Frazers' Edge.com

JAKE COULDN'T WAIT TO SHARE
HIS GUARANTEED CURE FOR HICCUPS

I vowed not to waste any more time. Who cares if I missed a workout or didn't get enough sleep? And the hell with my hair. I had to make the most of every day. I had to stop saving myself for later. Because nobody is guaranteed a later.

After drinking gallons of water to flush the rest of the medication out of my system over the next few days, I had the mother of all epiphanies. I could have been in a psychiatric facility. I could have jumped in front of traffic. I could have leaped off a building. I could have shot myself (if I had a gun). I could easily be dead. My middle-aged life should have been easier than my father's old age—but it wasn't.

1. STICKS THERMOMETER IN BATH TO MAKE SURE HE WON'T SINGE HIS TOES

2. DONS GOGGLES WHEN EATING RICE KRISPIES IN CASE ONE OF THEM SNAP, CRACKLES OR POPS INTO HIS CORNEA

3. HAS AIRBAGS IN HIS SUIT

4. WEARS SPF 80 TO BED TO PROTECT AGAINST NIGHTLIGHT

A DAY IN THE LIFE OF MR. CAUTIOUS

Frazers'Edge.com

As soon as I regained my health, I spent hours every day writing. I wrote stand-up. I worked on new levels for uSuck. I wrote tons of cartoons—challenging my father to keep pace with my output. It was a particularly prolific period for us. The Tamiflu takeover was a wake-up call. I would find a way to turn this into a positive.

I had to.

Here are some of the emails I sent him. (You can see how each of these turned out at the end of the chapter.)

BAD HAIR DAYS FOR LINCOLN AND EINSTEIN
We see Lincoln and Einstein standing side-by-side.
Lincoln's hair is the exact shape of his top hat.
Einstein's hair is neatly combed and parted to one side.

THE SKYWRITER WHO RELIED ON SPELL-CHECK
We see a pair of airplanes over the NYC skyline. The larger, higher-flying plane is writing a message that says, "THE STATE FAIR WELLCOMES YOU." A second, smaller, lower-flying plane is underlining the word "WELLCOMES" in red.

SOMETIMES HAL'S ATTENTION TO DETAIL BACKFIRED
Then we see a man adding the word "THE" to a "BEWARE OF DOG" sign (in between the words 'of' and 'dog') with a pen. A dog near the sign is about to attack him.

AIR B-N-BEARD
Then we see a man with a giant beard and hear several voices coming from it.
Voice 1: "It's so spacious!"
Voice 2: "And warm!"
Voice 3: "I'm never leaving!"

CHESS REAL ESTATE
We see a bishop from a chessboard sitting in a chair at a real estate office. The bishop looks irritated as he says to the real estate agent: "I can only move diagonally."

BAD PODCASTS
We see a sign in the background that says "THREE GUYS CLEARING THEIR THROATS" and a trio of men seated behind microphones, each clearing their throats. (*Herrrhem, Ahemmmm, Rrrrrrgggggg.*)

UNNECESSARY COMMERCIALS
Then we see a guy looking at us holding up a kidney and saying to camera, "Kidneys! You need at least one!"

REGGIE WASN'T THE MARKETING GENIUS HE THOUGHT HE WAS
Then we see a guy at a car dealership with a sign in the background that reads, "BUY 9 ROLLS ROYCES GET THE 10TH FREE!"
link to a Rolls Royce below (the key is to replicate the hood ornament)

KARAOKE WHISTLING DIDN'T SEEM TO CATCH ON
Then we see a man with his lips pursed whistling and a bunch of musical notes coming out of his mouth as the few confused patrons watching each have their own private thought bubbles as to what song the guy is whistling.
Customer 1: "Sweet Caroline?"
Customer 2: "Don't Stop Believing?"
Customer 3: "Gettin' Jiggy Wit it?"

NOTE: IT'S "WIT" NOT "WITH" SO THERE'S NO TYPO, DAD!

TAIL ENVY
Then we see a tail-less breed (such as a Rottweiler) walking past a dog with a large tail.

Rottweiler thinks to himself: "I wish I had one of those. Then no one could see my anal glands when I walk."

Link for Rottweiler but it could just be a generic tail-less dog!
http://cdn2.www.dogtime.com/assets/uploads/2011/01/file_22942_
rottweiler-460x290.jpg

A LITTLE LATE

We see a man holding up a monocle to his friend and saying the following:

"So instead of a single monocle I'd have TWO monocles joined together by
a tiny piece of plastic and then I'd build a device that would wrap around the
top of each ear!"

AND HERE'S HOW THE IDEAS TURNED OUT:

BAD HAIR DAYS FOR LINCOLN AND EINSTEIN

THE SKYWRITER
WHO RELIED ON SPELL-CHECK

—

SOMETIMES HAL'S ATTENTION TO
DETAIL BACKFIRED

AIR B-N-BEARD

—

BAD PODCASTS

—

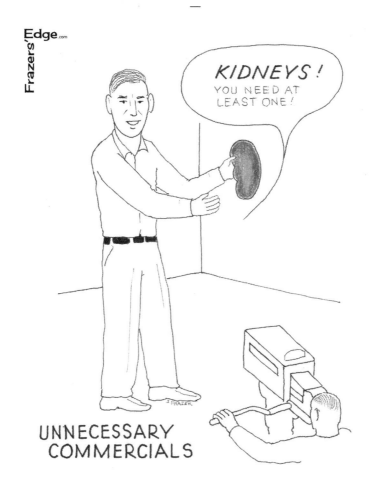

REGGIE WASN'T THE MARKETING GENIUS
HE THOUGHT HE WAS

KARAOKE WHISTLING DIDN'T SEEM TO CATCH ON

TAIL ENVY

A LITTLE LATE

I was officially embarrassed about my shame in not telling people at parties that my job was doing "cartoons with my dad." It wasn't "lame," it was great. Oh, well. I'll take growth any way I can.

CHAPTER 17
UNDAUNTED

While I was waiting for the uSuck coder to code and my cartooner to cartoon, I was also waiting for potential job leads to call me back.

My father wasn't waiting for anything. His priorities: painting and dating.

Rubble

The Uninvited Couple

He asked out someone in a parking lot, breaking the ice by telling her he liked the color of her bright yellow convertible. She said no.

He went on a date with his first gentile ever. She was from Nebraska and used to ride a horse to school. "Nice, but dull," my father told me.

He went out with a woman from J-Date in Naples who he said looked 97.

He went out with a woman Janice fixed him up with who she knew from her townhouse development. "She seemed to be surprised to be in public with a man," he told me when he got home, no malice in his voice, just dispensing info.

He finally clicked with a woman—but she was a snowbird so he ended it as soon as it started.

He asked out someone from his Chair Yoga class. Her husband had died many years ago and, assuming she'd be alone the remainder of her life, was so shocked another male had expressed any interest in her that she told my father she needed to think about it. She thought and eventually said no.

He went out with a woman whose husband had abruptly left her in the spring after twenty-five years—she was still trying to figure out why so she wasn't mentally available. Probably for the best.

He went out with someone named Evelyn who was "a cold fish with an impenetrable façade that doesn't allow for warmth." No, this wasn't Junot Díaz, these were my father's exact words.

He went out with a woman he really liked but it turned out she was Evelyn's best friend so that never got off the ground.

He went out with a Jewish woman whose Ukrainian ex-husband continued to tell her how much he hated Jews.

He asked out a woman at the end of a Silver Sneakers class. She was pressing her back against a wall of mirrors and sliding up and down to adjust her posture.
"I think you missed a spot," he said.
She chuckled.
"How about a cup of coffee sometime?" he continued.
"Okay."
They went out for coffee and one of the things that enticed her: my father's sense of humor in our cartoons.
"How old is she, Dad?"
"I don't know."
"But you've gone out with her three times already."
"I don't know."
"I'm surprised you asked what her name is."
"I didn't. She told me."
"I realize that you don't want to pry, Dad, but prying is part of dating."

Her name was Dorothy and things seemed promising. But they often do at the beginning. She had been a caretaker for her husband for the last five years of his life so my father and she had that in common.

"Dorothy is coming to temple with me on Friday."

"That's great, Dad! I didn't think she was Jewish."

"She's not. And I'm going to church with her on Sunday."

My father in a church was like... actually, if you remember, my rabbi quit our temple and became an Episcopalian Minister so my dad in a church was no big deal.

I still wasn't convinced this was leading anywhere until he announced that he wouldn't be able to do a cartoon tomorrow because he was "sleeping over."[35]

That was a big deal!

They spoke every day at the same time, they ate together nearly every day, exercised together. I'd say that they were inseparable except they each retained their own space. I was probably more delighted than he was.

I was planning another trip so I could meet Dorothy except when I told my father the dates I could come, he said that wasn't a good time.

"It's okay if you have activities during the day. I can amuse myself."

"No, I will be overseas."

"*Overseas?*"

"Dorothy and I are taking a trip to Greece, Spain, Italy and Israel."

CARTOGRAPHER'S BLOCK

Frazers' Edge.com

---

35   FYI it was nearly impossible for anyone to sleep over at my father's house unless she had the body of a pencil since he refused to upgrade the size of his twin bed.

My father had always wanted to go to Israel. This would be his first time in any foreign country other than Mexico (with Irene). But at 84, I was worried about him having the stamina for such an extensive trip.

"Dorothy is going to be able to handle all this?"

"Yes, she's a veteran world traveler."

"How old is she?"

"I don't know."

"C'mon! You're about to go halfway around the world with her! What do you mean, 'you don't know'?"

"I don't know."

"Have you asked her?"

I had no idea if he a) hadn't asked her because he didn't want to be intrusive; b) hadn't asked her because he didn't care how old she was; or c) had asked her and forgot the answer.

In any case, once you have someone's first and last name there are easy ways online to find out ages. Nancy is an online DOB sleuth. It took her less than ninety seconds to find out that Dorothy was 89. In the photos with my dad she looked closer to 65, a Shirley MacLaine look-alike with short red wavy hair and a killer smile. And, even though I still hadn't met her face-to-face, Debbie had and loved her. And Debbie's a tough nut to crack.

In the meantime, our coder hired some students at Sacramento State to help test uSuck. The good news was they were liking it but finding glitches. The bad news: Our release date kept getting pushed back.

I was on a conference call with the uSuck duo when I got a call on the other line. I assumed it was another telemarketer. It's always a telemarketer. I'm on every "no call" list in existence, which just makes me wonder how many worthless calls I'd get if I weren't. So whenever I answer the phone and I don't know who it is I spew indistinguishable gibberish. I'm hoping that the telemarketer will then mark off a box that indicates "doesn't speak English" and I'll be off the list. Particularly if they can't discern what language it is you're speaking and it's obviously not Spanish.

REGGIE HAD NO IDEA WHY BUSINESS
WAS SO BAD

"Trjsjhrayygalrarkekeksahh!"
"Hello?"
"Pyeyaktahhydckkwawa... Eaygiakdygaldlslsaiikdhhgdsa!"
"Hello? Brian?"
"Yes."
"I'm in Crete. I'm safe. I have to go now."

The entire conversation was twenty-nine seconds—70% of which was me making stupid noises—but when I heard my father's voice it felt like NASA's rover had landed on Mars. My dad had (*finally!*) made it to Europe! Anything on his bucket list was automatically on mine.

My euphoria was crushed by the time he got to Jerusalem. Dorothy emailed Debbie some pictures. Most of those were of my father in a wheelchair. At first I thought he'd had an accident. He hadn't. It was just age and fatigue. He looked old and frail, something I'd never associated with him. He'd always been a bull, a rock, a pillar of strength with giant Popeye forearms. This freaked me out. What would happen if he (finally) needed someone to take care of him? Would Dorothy stick by him? After all, she was on her way to ninety and had just done five years of caretaking. Would she just cut her losses and walk away? The person in the wheelchair was unrecognizable. The person in the wheelchair was an imposter, a cheaply made doppelganger. The person in the wheelchair was vulnerable. My dad was invulnerable, a veritable superhero. Superheroes didn't die.

Frazers'
Edge .com

I wondered if my father being wheelchair bound was karmic payback. One of the few arguments I get into with him is his liberal use of his handicapped placard, especially in Florida where so many elderly people genuinely need a closer, extra-convenient parking spot. In the past he's had knee troubles where the placard was a necessity. And having one while transporting my mother around was a must. But why would my father—the proud owner of a Fitbit, the man who was always moving his feet around under tables as if he were Gregory Hines, the long-time husband of a woman who was actually handicapped—use one when he wasn't?

Dorothy and my dad had been back from their trip for about a week but still hadn't sent me any pictures and, frankly, I was nervous to see any. We had spoken on the phone since but if the Jerusalem photos were any indication, a physical tipping point might have been reached. I was bracing for the worst — witnessing my father's health markedly decline—as Nancy and I planned a visit for the end of the month.

Three days later, I received an email from my father. It contained a link, which he had never done. I thought it might be a corrupt file but there was also a personal note so I clicked on it. There, in a suit and tie, was my (non-wheelchair sitting) father in front of his temple congregation—with Dorothy by his side—robustly announcing their engagement! Not only did my dad not look like he was going to be an invalid anytime soon, but he actually looked stronger, peppier, and more rejuvenated than I had seen him in years. I was so relieved to see him standing on his own that I nearly forgot the reason for the video. My father had a fiancé! They showed off their engagement rings—which the videographer-slash-guy-with-a-cell-phone failed to zoom in on—but I would see them in person on their hands soon enough.

When Nancy and I arrived at my father's I thought we had walked into the wrong place. It felt so... homey. It looked as if it was the "after" in a HGTV reality show. Following the death of my mother, my dad had begun to try to get rid of as many things as possible. He pulled the antique signs off the walls and sent them to various auctions. He gave away any furniture he didn't need to charities. He downsized his dining room and kitchen tables. He was trying to be as Spartan as possible to make it easy on us "so we wouldn't have to sift through piles of garbage when he was gone." Although thoughtful, this gesture made his house look barren, as if several roommates had just moved out, or he had just moved in and the moving van had broken down on the highway. The blank walls and lack of furnishings just made the dirt and filth stand out. It was depressing. But now... now the walls were alive with my father's art—his paintings, cartoons, and colored pencil drawings all expertly framed and mounted.

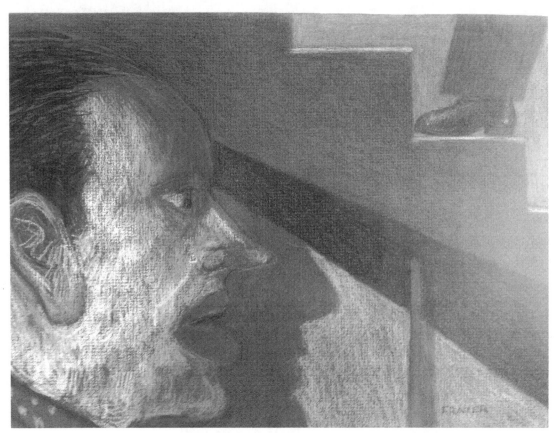

A trio of colored pencil drawings. This one is "Man Under the Steps"

Mr. Accordion

Children of Long Ago

There were throw pillows on the couch. There was a recliner where he could read. There was a small area rug. I hardly recognized the place from pre-Dorothy. This felt like a home (again), not an abandoned warehouse.

"Dad this is great!"

"Dorothy did it all! She always wanted to be an interior decorator."

Irene had done a makeover on my father, now Dorothy had done one on his house.

We picked Dorothy up at her complex, a lengthy twenty-five-minute drive — which is a lot of daily commuting for people eighty-plus. My father got out and met her at the elevator, where they kissed and held hands, giggling like school kids as they walked across the asphalt towards us. Because I had seen numerous photos of her, I knew what she looked like but I still couldn't believe she was nearly ninety. She walked comfortably on her own, wore large sunglasses and her skin had very little wear on it for her age. She was sharp, had a great sense of humor and spoke with confidence. Her hair looked effortlessly coiffed and she wore a stylish blazer.

Since Nancy and I love to ask questions, we did. Dorothy was a former opera singer. She had moved to Ft. Myers 25 years ago because a lot of her friends from up north had. (And several lived in her development, which is how she chose her apartment.) She had a daughter in Ohio. Her grandkid was about to move to Colorado. She had a red Prius. It was a relaxing and wonderful drive and Dorothy navigated the entire trip without any GPS, all from memory.

She insisted on taking us to her favorite restaurant next to a small lighthouse on the beach. It was very romantic, even though it was 11:30 in the morning.

My dad ordered a hot black coffee and a straw.

"What's the straw for, Dad?"

"The coffee. It stains the teeth less when you drink it this way." He proudly said he'd learned that from Dorothy.

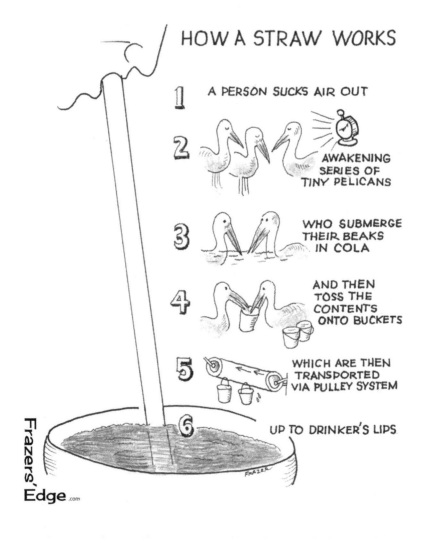

HOW A STRAW WORKS

1 A PERSON SUCKS AIR OUT

2 AWAKENING SERIES OF TINY PELICANS

3 WHO SUBMERGE THEIR BEAKS IN COLA

4 AND THEN TOSS THE CONTENTS ONTO BUCKETS

5 WHICH ARE THEN TRANSPORTED VIA PULLEY SYSTEM

6 UP TO DRINKER'S LIPS

Frazers' Edge .com

At the adjacent table were a shirtless guy and his girlfriend. I don't understand anyone who wants to eat without a shirt on. It's just weird. You're eating all these greasy things like curly fries and drinking beer and you care so little about yourself that you don't mind watching your stomach expand in front of a crowd? I mean, seriously, dude! I'm about to pay $28 for a lunch entrée—how about I toss in another $6 for a T-shirt for you?!

When our food arrived, my father and Dorothy held hands and said a little prayer. Which made me uncomfortable. He had never done that before in his life and I remained uneasy with religion. On the other hand, what was wrong with being thankful for your food? I didn't believe that God would actually hear your appreciation, but it certainly wasn't harming anyone. And better to be thankful than not. The problem was with me, not them.

"When are you getting married?" Nancy chimed in.
"Oh, we don't have a date set yet," they replied, nearly in unison.
"But Dorothy and I might be going on a trip to Hawaii soon."
"That's where Nancy and I had our honeymoon."
"We'll try to stop off in Los Angeles to spend a few days with you," he said, his eyes lovingly meeting his soon-to-be-bride.

I could barely contain myself. My father had never been further west in America than Mobile, Alabama and that was in 1962 on a National Science Foundation Stipend. I couldn't wait to take both of them around to all the sights—the dog park under the Hollywood Sign, the Walk of Fame, Dodger Stadium, the sushi place with the eagle's nest view of the city. I began mentally planning every facet of their trip. Which hotel they'd stay at, which restaurants we'd eat at, which tours we'd go on. Their entire layover would be on me, as a wedding/engagement present. In fact, if it all worked out, maybe he could have an exhibit while he was in Los Angeles? Dozens of my friends had said they wanted to meet him and buy some of his paintings. It was just a question of how to transport his work across the country. And he'd have to do it piecemeal, so in case something got lost or damaged his entire collection wouldn't be gone.

Throughout the rest of the meal my mind kept leaping from the present into the future. I never dreamt that my father would get on a plane and fly 3,000 miles to visit me in California. I never imagined him remarried. I never imagined him getting artistic recognition for his paintings. I never imagined him jubilant.

It was a miracle. I felt like joining hands with Nancy and thanking God for giving him the opportunity to visit me. I said a silent "thanks" in my head as Dorothy picked up the check and shirtless man belched so loudly people in Tampa could hear.

CHAPTER 18
A FINAL COAT OF PAINT

> WAKE UP AND GET INTO POSITION! THE IDIOTS ARE COMING TO STARE AT US SOON!

STONEHENGE AFTER A NIGHT OF PARTYING

This sentence will not seem very exciting to you.

My father is having a party at his house.

My father has never had a party at his house. Because it's impossible to have a party when there are no other people.

The only other person besides Irene and Dorothy (not including his computer guy or occasional housekeeper) to even break the plane of his front door was his sex addict next-door neighbor Dan—to change a light bulb. Even when I was growing up on Long Island, the most outsiders simultaneous in our house were two. (Usually Mr. and Mrs. Stier who were there solely for business to trade antiques with my mother, which was hardly a party.)

Part of Dorothy's (long-term) goal in helping my father redecorate the place was so he could finally have people over. Now they were throwing a party to commemorate the one-year anniversary of their first date. The majority of my father's guest list would be from his temple. Dorothy's friends—many of whom he'd be meeting for the first time—would make up the rest of the invitees.

The party was scheduled for a Sunday afternoon from two to five.

"Are you supplying any liquor, Dad?"

"There will be a bottle of Manischewitz." He assumed Nancy and I were the only people on the planet interested in alcohol.

"Does that even count as liquor? For how many people?"

"I don't know. Twenty? Twenty-five?"

"Shouldn't you at least pick up a bottle of scotch or some chardonnay?"

"Nah."

"What kind of food are you serving?"

"I don't know. I will have to discuss it with Dorothy."

Based on the liquor menu, I wouldn't have been surprised if the eating portion of the party was comprised of a bag of baby carrots and jar of mayo.

DINNER PARTY FAUX PAS # 487

The day after the party, my father sent me pictures. It felt as if everything was Photoshopped. There were actual adults in his dining room holding beverages[36] in their hands! There were actual adults in his kitchen conversing! There were actual adults in his living room chewing! Debbie and Jon were there, as was Dan, so I wouldn't have to hire a notary to verify that there were bona fide social interactions taking place in my dad's house.

"You had people over! How did it feel?!" I was now speaking to my father as if he were a thirteen-year-old with Asperger's.

"It was nice."

"Are you planning another party?"

"Possibly."

My father's blossoming was complete.

"When are you going to Hawaii? I can't wait to show you around Los Angeles!"

There was a long pause on the phone as my father cleared his throat as if doing a lame machine gun impression. I knew something wasn't right.

"We had to cancel Hawaii."

"What? Why?"

"Because I won't be able to deal with any luggage. I may need an operation on my rotator cuff."

Frazers'Edge

---

36   Non-alcoholic

It's embarrassing to admit but my first thoughts were selfish: "No more cartoons for a while?!" I had been in silent jerk mode for quite some time now. Instead of relishing each and every moment of happiness Dorothy (and the rest of his ever-evolving lifestyle) was providing him, I was only focused on our cartoon output. How many cartoons was he behind? Why did he have to go see that musical downtown when it had been ten days since he last sent me a sketch?

The cartoon-manufacturing part of my brain switched itself off since there was no point in creating something that would rarely be inked in and hence, never seen. I was in constant nagging mode with him and the less he sketched the more I nagged. I realized I was more reliant on our cartoons than I thought. It wasn't purely artistic motives. The more cartoons we created the more micro-stories I would preserve in my head. This gave me comfort for when my father was no longer around. I would not only have emotional memories, but visual proof as well.

"I had no idea you had any shoulder problems. When did this happen?"
"It's been bothering me for a while."
"When is the operation?"
"I'm not sure. Debbie wants me to get a second opinion. But we had to cancel the trip."

THE HUNCHBACK OF NOTRE DAME
GETS A SECOND OPINION

I was devastated. I had a feeling he would never make it out West. All of his traveling was suspended indefinitely. I thought of telling him to come out anyway—luggage-less—and to just pack toiletries and he could wear my baggy clothes when he got here. Or to mail me the clothes he wanted to wear and then I'd mail them back. Or to pack super light. Our friends Steve and Julie go away for a month and have such a great packing system it looks like they're just going on a picnic for an hour.

My father already had an appointment with a surgeon. Fortunately, it was his right shoulder so he'd still be able to draw and paint. Unfortunately, he was 84 now and 84-year-old parts don't heal so easily.

The second doctor recommended a cortisone injection in his shoulder combined with physical therapy and then they'd revisit the operation scenario in a few weeks. But he, too, implored my father to avoid lifting or carrying anything. Any semblance of travel would be forbidden.

I was heartbroken—for both of us.

In the meantime I bought him a present.

My dad had spoken about mailing some Holocaust museums "a disk" of his paintings to see if they were interested in displaying any of his work. I had to explain to him that people don't mail each other "disks" anymore and that most computers don't even have a slot to insert a "disk." Instead you just email whomever you're trying to contact and give them a link to your pieces. It was time to get my father his own website, separate from FrazersEdge.

I gave him a list of available options that contained his name. He decided on:

TheArtOfSamFrazer.com

"So I can put my own paintings up online?"
"Absolutely! I'll talk you through every step."
He was excited to branch out. I was even more excited that I could help him.

He would now be fully in control of the input and output of his creations. If he felt like painting for ten minutes he could do that. If he felt like painting for ten hours he could do that. He could invest all of his emotions into whatever he chose, unencumbered by my emails of our cartoons.

Once he approved the layout and design I could start contacting museums and galleries—disk-less!—and see if they would show his work. However, I wasn't able to share the prototype with him. He wasn't answering his phone. No text responses. Voice mail only on his landline and cell. No email replies, even to brief messages that required one-word answers. I was worried. I called Debbie to make sure he was okay.

"Oh, he's fine. He's on a cruise to the Cayman Islands with Dorothy."

"I thought he wasn't supposed to travel?"

"He probably shouldn't have but the tickets were non-refundable."

We spoke at least once a day and he never mentioned a word about a cruise. Did he just forget? Or did he not want me to discourage him from going because of his shoulder? Or maybe he just felt like being a little sneaky. In any case, part of me felt hurt and betrayed and another part of me admired him for being such a rapscallion.

I'd always considered myself a risk-taker. I went out on the road and did stand-up for ten years. I voluntarily dressed up as a robot and performed without a microphone in an airplane hangar. I powerlifted and bodybuilded despite having a slight frame that urged I do neither. But, in reality, I am insanely conservative.

I wouldn't take a chance on having kids because I was afraid I wouldn't be able to support them. I wouldn't lease a new car because I didn't want to take on any car payments or responsibility. My 1988 Volvo with the cassette player and roll-up windows was plenty good for me. I didn't want to have my shitty driveway repaved because it might attract undue attention to our house. I was a settler, unwilling to take the leap necessary to have a better life. I thought about my days back in Little League. I played baseball from age eight to about fifteen and I can't remember ONE SINGLE TIME sliding into a base. Not once. I was afraid if I slid my cleats would get caught in the dirt and I'd get hurt or get hit in the head with an errant throw.

My dad had evolved into the real risk taker. Going on a cruise with a damaged rotator cuff. Asking out women in awkward situations because he was willing to accept rejection if there was even a .000001% chance of her saying "yes." Getting on a plane even though he wasn't crazy about heights. Getting on a boat even though he feared water and couldn't swim. Risking his emotions at eighty-four, knowing that, at any given moment, his heart could be broken (again).

My father was back from the cruise, his shoulder no worse off than when he'd left. He approved of the website I'd set up and was already telling all his friends to click. In the meantime, I was getting tired of waiting for everyone to get back to me about his paintings. I had left three messages with one gallery, five messages with another. I called or emailed Holocaust museums daily. I couldn't even get a single person to look at his art, much less reject it. I wasn't asking anyone to read a novel or a screenplay. Just spend ten seconds, check out the website and scroll down. If you don't like the first three paintings, stop scrolling and delete the link.

My frustration grew deeper with every day of silence. To quote the great Bill Marich[37]: "I gotta make something happen!" In reality, transporting all my father's work—and his bum shoulder—out West would be too much. My new plan was to rent out a local gallery in Florida for his paintings to be displayed. He could sell signed lithographs and prints. I would even hire a cameraman to document the event.

As I was multi-tasking, Googling places to rent out in Ft. Myers while I continued my barrage of phone calls, I miraculously got a curator on the phone.

"Hi, I'm Sam Frazer's son, Brian. I had sent you a couple of emails with a link to his paintings."

"Oh. I don't think I ever received it."

"I wrote 'Sam Frazer Paintings' in the subject header."

"And when did you do this?"

"Last week. And the week before that. Hang on, I'll send it to you again right now, just in case it keeps going to spam. I can wait if you wanna make sure you got it."

"Sure. Hold on. Yes, I got it. Let me look at it and why don't you call me in an hour?"

"Okay. Thanks!"

I didn't expect her to open the link when we hung up and I certainly didn't expect her to answer her phone when I called back but I was happily wrong on both accounts.

"I would LOVE to have your father's work shown here!"

"Well... he would LOVE to show it there!" I was speaking so loudly I bet the douchebags across the cul-de-sac could hear me.

"I'll go through my calendar and email you and him with some potential dates."

"Fantastic!" I could feel the curator pulling the phone away from her ear to reduce my volume.

---

37   Okay, he's not actually that great. Just a friend of mine I wanted to give a shout-out to.

THE AUCTIONEER
WHO WANTED TO BEAT TRAFFIC

I had chills running down my spine and goosebumps filled my arms and I hadn't even called my father yet.

"Dad! I got you an exhibit!" I was now officially screaming.

"Really? Where?!?!"

"Chipotle! The third stall in the woman's bathroom but it's a start! Actually it's a place in downtown Ft. Myers called *The White Gallery*." For Holocaust paintings? Hello, irony.

"*The White Gallery*!?"

"Yes, I know, it sounds a little racist. You can go and meet the gallery curator next week if you want. She loves your work! And you can show up to twenty-five paintings and she'll help you decide what to charge."

"Thank you for doing this."

"You did all the hard work. I just nagged some strangers."

The joy in my father's voice resonated throughout my body. I felt far happier helping him achieve this goal than when I achieved something on my own. Maybe it was because, for all my obscurity and lack of financial success, I realized I had already completed mine. I wanted to be a professional stand-up. I was. I wanted to record a punk album in England. I did. I wanted to be a comedy writer in Hollywood. Check. I wanted to write for Esquire Magazine. Yes. I wanted to be a published author. I was. I wanted to create a videogame. I did.[38] Basically, every artistic endeavor I had pursued in life I had attained. For the past three and a half decades it had all been about me. Now, at fifty-four, maybe it was time to pass the "recognition" torch not to a younger generation, but to an older one. There must be other elderly people out there like my father who wanted to be acknowledged before it was too late.

I imagined the forgotten impressionist in Duluth; the ignored cubist in Provo; the neglected landscape artist in Bangor who defined himself by his pre-retirement day job.

My spirits were soaring. While at a party, I was showing a relative of Nancy's my father's website on my phone as I told her how he had taken all this time off and now had some museums and galleries interested in his work. She showed me a photo on her phone of one of her friends, Cora, who was in her early eighties and did these amazing wire sculptures. I asked for her contact info.

Sure, the satisfaction I would get from helping a stranger wouldn't match what it felt like to help my dad, however it would still feel pretty fulfilling. And pushing someone else's creative wares would be a lot easier than trying to push my own. You have carte blanche to praise someone else's work effusively. You sound like a pretentious conceited jackass praising yourself. Of course, I still planned on continuing my own creative endeavors but this could be mutually rewarding.

Why is it important if my father, or anyone else, has his or her work discovered? Because—fame or no fame—one of the most important human desires is to feel important. To feel significant. To feel loved. To feel like your existence matters (to someone or somebody). That's why my father's life was particularly cruel to me. He was a caretaker for years—by nature, a job, under optimal conditions, bordering on awful—and never once did my mother make him feel the importance or significance he deserved. Whether or not he felt loved... well... that's his call. That her behavior shut off the spigots on both of his importance taps—personal and artistic—made it an even worse fate. I remember when my first book came out in 2007. It didn't sell a lot of copies but the press was very favorable. I was on

---

38   Hopefully by the date of publication uSuck will be available for downloads.

Entertainment Weekly's Must List, *USA Today* gave it glowing reviews, as did *The Daily News* and *New York Post*. But what I'll remember the most is two people, two strangers, contacting me via Facebook to tell me how much they loved the book. I remember both of their names to this day. One identified with my anger issues and neuroses. The other also grew up with a mother with M.S. who tore apart their family. I will never forget either one.

Sometimes a compliment is the only compensation you need. But you can't receive that if you're working in a vacuum with no witnesses.

Oddly, one of the reasons my fame quotient is satisfied is because of my mother. She encouraged my every artistic endeavor. She made me feel beyond significant. She made me feel special. Once I had a taste of accolades from strangers I no longer had anything to prove to anyone. Certainly not to my parents—which is a common motivator for standing out and getting famous.

"Dad, guess what?"

"*The White Gallery* is only allowing me to use white paint in my exhibit?"

"Close. You've inspired me to help other older artists besides you get recognized. It'll be like the movie *Field of Dreams* but with art. Instead of 'If You Build it, He Will Come,' it'll be 'If You Create It, They Will See It.'" Hopefully.

"That's wonderful. Very few people try to reach their full potential."

"Have you?"

"I think so. I'm certainly trying," he said. "I feel like my potential is soaring. I feel very uninhibited and free. You see... I believe that there's no ceiling for potential. A lot of it is self-motivation."

"Obviously I'll still keep pushing other galleries for you and help you get ready for your opening."

"I figured that."

"And we'll still do cartoons here and there."

"Of course."

"Hey... I've been meaning to ask... do you resent not being able to sink yourself into art for all those years you were taking care of mom?"

"No. Because from a curse can come a blessing. I'm very happy now."

Even though I was flying into Ft. Myers next month, it was my father who had arrived.

And that was how the book was supposed to end. But then, a few days before my publisher's deadline, I got a phone call in the middle of the night.

"Dad's in the hospital." It's Debbie, who never calls after nine. "If the ambulance came five minutes later he would've died. Heart attack plus congestive heart failure."

I had spoken to him earlier that day and he seemed fine. Although it was odd that the cartoon he'd sent was missing the last word ("player")—rendering it meaningless.

Frazers'Edge.com

IT WAS DIFFICULT TO TELL WHO WAS
THE BETTER AIR HARMONICA

When I told him about the omission he said that he'd "fix it later."

"You better get down here," Debbie says. "I'm looking into hospice care now but it doesn't look good. I'm not sure he's even gonna make it out of the hospital."

My sister, unfortunately, has a good track record predicting death. She heard the death rattle in my mother within eight hours of her passing.

She tells me that he will either need to have a series of stents or open-heart surgery. Either way, operating on an 85-year-old isn't ideal. Then, assuming he survives one of the procedures, he'll have to be transferred to another hospital where he'll need an aortic valve replaced. Oh, and if he doesn't do any of these things, he will be what is known as a "Cardiac Cripple." That means that his combination of dizziness, fainting and loss of breath could lead to a heart attack at any given moment—while driving, walking down a supermarket aisle, shaving, anytime. As my sister, the nurse, so eloquently puts it, "He'll be a walking time bomb."

To pile on the irony, earlier that day Mark had forwarded me a video that a friend of his had seen online. It was a commercial for a chain of health clubs. "Check out the clip @ 1:46" I was told.

"I would recommend this facility to any person regardless of age because they have so many different kinds of activities."

I didn't need to read the chyron because I recognized the face. It was my father. And he looked exceedingly vibrant and healthy. And it had to have been shot fairly recently because the video had just been posted.

I buy a one-way ticket to Florida. The flight feels so long I wonder if the pilot is flying through New Zealand to get to Ft. Myers. As the plane bumps and glides through turbulence and clouds, I rewind my father's life. Although we hadn't met until 1964, I knew his first 31 years were filled with promise—he'd had a loving childhood and happy early marriage. Then he hit a 35-year rough patch. I had expected him to sadly die before my mother, but his final act has turned out better than my siblings and I could have imagined. He has been playing with house money for nearly half a decade. I rationalize that, no matter what happens to him now, he will die a winner.

Since he's in the hospital, there will be plenty of meds to control the pain and hopefully he will have a quick ending, free from suffering.

Although my dad and I never said we loved each other, it's implied. Our daily talks more than covered those three words. If we never spoke again, I rationalized that I could hold my head high. Though far from a perfect person, I am confident that I am a good son. When I commuted weekly from Boston to New York to do the comedy clubs, I always stopped at home and made sure to cut the lawn—because I knew my father was already over-extended. I'd walk the dog. Load the dishwasher. Anything that would take even the smallest task off his plate. I'd try to run some errands for him or, even better, tag along while he ran them so he'd have company. He has always been my best friend, whether he knows it or not.

And it's not like 85 isn't a good run. Especially for someone whose main source of calories for decades was junk food. Most people on the planet don't make it to 85, especially men. The biggest sadness for me is that my mother— blinded by her illness—never recognized how lucky she was to have married my dad.

When I get off the plane I immediately call Debbie.
"Is he still alive?"
"Barely."
"Shit."
"I know. It's bad, Brian. It's really bad. The blockage in his arteries was 90%."
"Shit."
"Just do me a favor and when you visit don't joke around with him. He has to conserve what little strength he has left."
"Okay."

I walk into his hospital room. He is snoring with his mouth open and has oxygen tubes in his nose and desperately needs a shave. My brother Mark often grows a beard or a mustache, but neither my dad nor I ever had a semblance of facial hair—not even an accidental soul patch from erratic shaving. So it's odd to see all his gray hairs poking out from his cheeks, chin and upper lip. I'm glad to see him breathing but this is more upsetting than I'd imagined. His forehead seems to have picked up an additional wrinkle or two. Each of his inner forearms are black and blue from all the tubes inserted and blood taken, his hospital gown even more ill-fitting than expected. I want to take a picture to send to Mark and Stacey to show that he's okay, but this isn't exactly a great photo-op.

After a few minutes, a nurse enters to check his oxygen levels and he wakes. "How are you feeling, Dad?" He adjusts his eyes until he sees that it's me. "Not bad. But I think my roller-skating days might be over." His energy is a lot more positive than I had expected. I spot a napkin with some doodling on the back on his food tray.

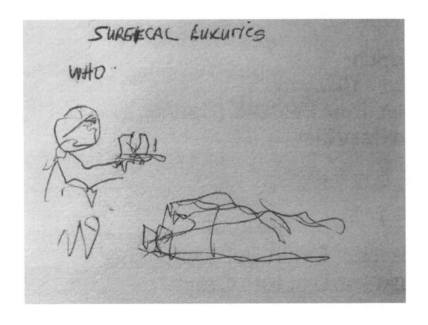

"Oh, Brian... listen, I've been thinking of some cartoons."

I stare down at the back of the napkin. It's a surgeon performing an operation on a patient. The caption says, "Surgical Luxuries." I'm elated that he already feels a need to be creative.

"It's great that you're able to draw. What's your idea?"

"Somebody could be bringing a surgeon a drink and say, 'I have your latte here,' or whatever the drinks are called. I don't know the coffee jargon. Then the surgeon could say, 'But I ordered something else.' Whatever that may be. Then maybe the nurse comes in and says, 'You forgot my croissant!' And so on."

"Maybe the anesthesia hasn't worn off yet, Dad. But that's even worse than usual." Although I think his "and so on" addition is hilarious. But he's talking! And drawing! I didn't think he'd ever do either.

Actually, there is no anesthesia. The surgeon had gone in through his groin to insert the stents and, because of my father's age and thin blood, they couldn't put him under. Instead he has been loaded up with Valium.

A nurse walks in to take his blood pressure.

"This is my son, Brian. He just flew in from California!"

"Oh, very nice. What time is it in there now?" That's an odd question but okay.

"It's three o'clock here so it's noon on the West Coast," I respond.

"Oh, it's earlier there?"

I answer with a curt "yes" and change the subject. *You don't know HOW TIME WORKS and you're in charge of my father's vitals?*

"I wonder how much I'm gonna get for my gown on eBay?" my dad jokes with the nurse. "Probably not very much."

This is the opposite of my mother in the hospital. 100% positive. Upbeat. Confident. A lover of life. A room that the nurses don't try to avoid. My father has the perfect attitude to have in a medical facility. Anywhere, actually.

He is laughing at everything.
Laughing at the doctor's jokes.
Laughing at his own jokes.
Laughing at Geico commercials.

Laughing—even though Debbie doesn't want him to.

His laugh now sounds exactly like my grandfather's—although it hadn't always. Laughs evolve. I was probably already on my fifth or sixth different laugh since college. I wonder if my grandfather had passed his laugh onto my dad before his death. And, if so, would my laugh someday sound like my father's?

"Dad, how about this for a cartoon? 'The World's Worst Cardiologist' Then we see a doctor operating on someone and he says, 'This heart looks terrible. Good thing everyone has two!'"

He laughs.

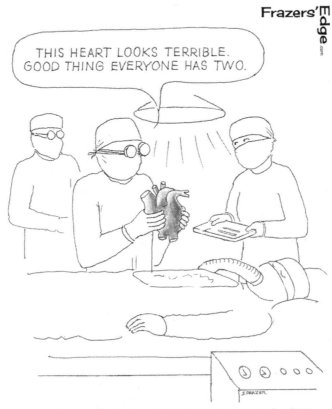

THE WORLD'S WORST CARDIOLOGIST

After eleven days, I'm finally allowed to drive him home. The nurse tells me the general rule is that for each day in the hospital you need five days to recover. That would mean 55 days.

"Dad, do you think you'll be able to do your exhibit in June?"

"I don't know." He seems skeptical, not because of his health but because "people [aka art gallery owners] frequently back out and renege on deals."

His life will be far different than eleven days ago. He'll require oxygen twenty-four hours a day, a walker, a collection of new medications and a new diet. He'll also have to get on a scale daily—to ensure that his weight drops because if it doesn't it means the fluids in his body aren't leaving. He'll need to blow into a plastic bong-like device to record his breathing power every waking hour. He'll have to sleep on his back at a forty-five-degree angle with his legs slightly elevated to help drain the fluids in his feet. Debbie buys him a special bed that enables him to retain the shape of a Pringles potato chip.

He will require a fleet of nurses, nurse practitioners, occupational therapists, physical therapists and social workers. I'm in charge of him and have been given strict orders. If his groin starts to bleed, put pressure on it and call 911 immediately. Make sure there's nothing on the ground he can trip over. Make sure he's always connected to his oxygen—of which there are forty-seven feet of tubes so it reaches every corner of the house. Make sure he takes his morning pills in the morning and his evening pills at night. Make sure he doesn't have any sodium or salt in his diet.

If all this sounds overwhelming, you'd be wrong. I welcome it. I'm grateful he's alive and so is he.

"I'm functioning fine," he assures me. "It's just in slow-motion."

The toughest thing for him is not being able to see Dorothy as much as he'd like. She's currently in the midst of a series of lens operations so, at least for now, isn't able to drive. But she has taken cabs to visit him in the hospital daily and they speak twice a day. Although they still have no wedding date, he delights in referring to her as his fiancé. His signature sign-off to her on the phone: "I love you dear and have a good night. G'bye sweetie. Bye bye."

The hardest thing for me is the oxygen machine. I'm a misophone which means I'm very sensitive to sounds. This sound in particular triggers me. And, yes, I know the noises are helping keep my father alive but that doesn't mean it doesn't simultaneously annoy me. The machine releases a loud clang every other second (yes, 30x a minute!) that sounds as if someone in the house is using a giant stapler. It's like Big Ben is a metronome. It's like a mechanical monkey slamming a pair of cymbals together—except the monkey is using frying pans. Debbie brings me earplugs but still the echo-y clangs cut through. I would rather be subjected to the constant sounds of our overweight friends farting inches away from my ears 24/7 than this oxygen nonsense.

I try to make my father laugh as much as possible. Whenever he's sitting at the kitchen table and a new health worker comes over, I casually put a beer in front of him.

"What are you doing, Brian?"

"Oh, please, Dad! Don't pretend you're not drunk by 10:30 every morning!"

My father always shoots me a look of scorn while hiding a laugh.

One afternoon there is some loud banging on the front door.

I run to answer it. It's my dad's neighbor, Dan.

"Are you guys okay?" Dan asks nervously.

"Sure. Why?"

Dan points to the driveway.

"That."

"Oh, that's the nurse," I tell him.

"The friggin' nurse? I thought you were being robbed!"

The nurse[39] trying to prevent my father from having another heart attack nearly gave his neighbor one.

She gives my father the "old people falling" lecture. "Try not to fall." Who *tries* to fall? I mean, other than a stuntman. And how about *you* try not to drive something the size of a Panzer tank, you gas-guzzling, vision-blocking pixie? But of course I say nothing. She's helping keep my father alive and willingly changed the bandages on his groin.[40]

Every hour I remind my father to blow into the plastic bong-looking device.
He treats it as if it were that amusement park strength game where you have to pummel a target at the base with a mallet to see how high you can propel something.
"I got it up to 1500 [units]!" he announces proudly.
He could barely hit 500 when we first got back home.

He turns everything into a game.

He talks back to the talking scale after recording his weight.
"Your weight is one-hundred... and... eighty-seven... point ... five... pounds," the piece of plastic on the floor informs him.
"Your... feet... are... very... dirty..." he repeats in the scale's identical staccato. "Please... wash... them... in... the... next... month."

My father doesn't have caller ID on his landline so he never knows who he's going to speak to.
"Hello?"
And he begins to laugh hysterically.
"Who was it?"
"Another robo-call."
"Why is that funny?"

---

39   She was 5'4" and 125 lbs-ish so not even a large nurse.

40   Prediction: eventually, robots will do this.

"I don't know. It just makes me laugh when I hear 'This is an important message. Do not hang up the phone.' Wouldn't it make more sense to say 'Do not hang up the phone. This is an important message'?"

"Maybe. But I bet you're the only person on the planet who laughs when a computer calls and annoys you. To me, *that's* the funny."

Through physical therapy, a healthy diet, a joyful attitude and the fluids draining from his body he is dropping close to two pounds a day.

"Luck of the draw."

"What do you mean?"

"Luck of the draw that I got sick. Luck of the draw that I'm getting better. Luck of the draw."

For meals, we either order in or Debbie comes by to replenish the fridge, but after four days I feel a need to get out of the house for a quick supermarket run myself. I finally feel comfortable enough to leave my father alone. He's in his reclining chair with his head and feet in their medically mandated positions and assures me he doesn't have to go to the bathroom. The oxygen machine is whirring and I make sure the plugs are securely in his nose. The baseball game is on and the remote control and telephone are inches away from him, should he need either. The grocery store is just one traffic light and 1.2 miles away. I won't be gone long. I remind him that I'll have my phone turned on, and check that the volume is up full six times before I leave the house.

"See you in about a half-hour, Dad."

"Okay."

Twenty-six minutes later I'm back. The oxygen nose tubes are dangling from the side of the chair. My father is gone. Jesus Christ! I knew I shouldn't have left! I should have just had food delivered! I bet he fell in the bathroom—just like the Monster Truck nurse said he would even though he assured me he didn't have to go to the bathroom! I run to the bathroom. He's not there. Where the hell is he?! Debbie is gonna kill me. Maybe he went out to the lanai to look at ducks and fell down the hill into the lake and bled to death! I'm an idiot for leaving him alone and for wanting Kombucha that Debbie couldn't find even though I'd called Publix and they said they had it! Shit. He's not in his bed, either. Fuuuuuuuuuuuuuuuck!!!!!!

Then I sprint down the hallway and there he is, at his drafting table, drawing. He's fixing the caption on the harmonica cartoon he had sent me three weeks ago so it would finally make sense. To me, adding this lone word ("player") was more impressive than the ceiling of the Sistine Chapel.

"Jesus! I was so worried about you!"

"Why?"

"You were supposed to stay in your reclining chair until I got back. That was the plan."

"I don't like plans."

My father and I have done almost 1,000 cartoons together but this is by far my favorite, although it's neither the funniest nor the best drawn.

Frazers' Edge.com

IT WAS DIFFICULT TO TELL WHO WAS
THE BETTER AIR HARMONICA PLAYER

"I just have to scan this and send it to you."

"I have your dinner, Dad."

"I'll eat later. I want to at least do a rough sketch of the next one."

Although I ate alone, it's the happiest meal I've ever had.

END OF BOOK

ABOUT THE FONT

The font grew up in Wheeling, West Virginia and moved to Toledo, Ohio in 1989 where it lives with its same sex partner and three cats.